Also by Betty B. Osman

LEARNING DISABILITIES: A FAMILY AFFAIR

NO ONE TO PLAY WITH

The Social Side of Learning Disabilities

NO ONE TO PLAY WITH

The Social Side of Learning Disabilities

BETTY B. OSMAN

in association with
Henriette Blinder

RANDOM HOUSE NEW YORK

All rights reserved under International and Pan-American Copyright
Conventions.
Published in the United States by Random House, Inc., New York,
and
simultaneously in Canada by Random House of Canada Limited,
Toronto.

Library of Congress Cataloging in Publication Data

Osman, Betty B.
No one to play with—the social side of learning
disabilities.

Bibliography: p.
1. Learning disabilities—Social aspects. I. Blinder,
Henriette. II. Title.
LC4704.084   371.9   81-40241
ISBN 0-394-51134-4 AACR2

Manufactured in the United States of America
24689753
First Edition

TO AL

whose love and encouragement
have made my work possible

A NOTE

For many youngsters with learning differences, the real disability is not the reading or math problem, but the handicap that isolates them from their peer group. It has taken professionals a long time to recognize what parents have always known—that the learning-disabled child often just doesn't "fit in." He cannot get along with his peers in the classroom *or* on the playground.

This book will describe what makes it so hard for these children to get along in their world and suggest ways parents, teachers, and other caregivers can help them with their social as well as their academic problems. The suffering of the present generation of learning-disabled (LD) adults, only recently recognized, can probably be minimized by earlier attention to the social side of learning disabilities.

I would like to express my gratitude to the children and the families with whom I have worked. Through their courage and perseverance in searching for solutions to their problems, they have contributed immeasurably to this book. In addition, several individuals have been particularly helpful: my thanks to Bill Tarplin, M.S.W., Dr. Barry Singer, Benice Jackler, Lynda Getlan, Arthur Lipper, Mike D'Amore, Jody Dichek, Charlotte Mayerson, my editor, and, of course, my family—for their continued support. To all those who have so generously shared their experiences with me, personally or through correspondence, I am deeply grateful.

Most of all, to my associate and close friend, Henriette Blinder, my eternal thanks. Her creativity and insight, her fund of knowledge, and her experience in the field made her an invaluable partner. The process of writing this book together with her was an enriching experience personally as well as professionally.

CONTENTS

Introduction

THE PROBLEM

In the past ten or fifteen years, learning disabilities have become a major educational concern in this country. A child is considered to have a learning disability (rather than to be intellectually impaired) if he has extreme difficulty in certain areas of learning that do not seem commensurate with his ability. Thanks to federal legislation, nationally organized parent groups and the commitment of professionals to improving the quality of education, schools are providing more services and programs than ever before to help youngsters for whom learning is difficult. Children are seen by learning-disability specialists and school psychologists for diagnosis and remedial help.

In light of this improvement in services, it is tempting for parents and educators who have fought for these programs to begin to feel that the battle has been won. They are assuming, though, that learning problems only affect a child's ability to master academic subjects. But it is becoming quite evident that learning disabilities, or to use a better term, learning differences, go beyond the three Rs. They create a multitude of social problems across the board for youngsters in their daily lives.

These "living disabilities" can become far more pervasive and anxiety-provoking for the child and his family than his problems with reading or math. A child can always carry a calculator to help solve arithmetic problems, or use a tape recorder to avoid taking notes in class, but there is no invention that can take him successfully through a classmate's birthday party or a family crisis at home. He may be much more worried about being left out of Saturday morning's baseball game than failing tomorrow's spelling test. While most children at some time or other feel "unpopular" and deserted by friends, for the child with learning disabilities this feeling is often the usual condition. He is likely to be the lonely youngster on the block with no one to play with.

Most children tend to mature rather evenly; their intellectual and social skills develop almost simultaneously, and they progress in both areas in fairly predictable stages. But children with learning differences frequently lag behind in their reading ability, and their social skills may also be significantly delayed. When an eight-year-old cries at the slightest insult, when a ten-year-old kicks and teases the dog, and when a twelve-year-old still has temper tantrums, parents become understandably upset. I have heard many of them cry in frustration and bewilderment, "Why can't he act his age?"

It may well be that whatever it is that causes a child to have difficulty in reading, spelling, and counting also affects his adjustment at home and on the playground. The delays that many children experience in perceiving, understanding, and reacting to life's events affect much more than their performance in the classroom. Their out-of-school lives and social relationships may also be out of synch. They may, for example, seem less mature than their classmates and lack good judgment. They may also be more egocentric than children their age usually are and therefore insensitive to the needs of others. For these and similar reasons, LD children are likely to be rejected by their peers. It is not surprising, then, that when learning in school is difficult, so too is learning to live in a social world.

A child lives in many places other than the classroom. He is judged, then punished or rewarded for his behavior by a world of people who help him form an image of himself. How a child feels about himself depends largely on the response he receives from everyone in his world. It is hard to realize how many social transactions even a young child has during the course of a day. Staying with baby sitters, calling a classmate for an assignment, trips to grandparents, family celebrations, going to the store or to camp, engaging in competitive sports—each can present difficulties for any child, but is particularly problematic for a child with learning differences.

Of course, not *all* children with learning disabilities have accompanying social problems. If a boy in our society is lucky enough to be a natural athlete, or if his athletic ability has been nurtured, his deficient academic skills may not seem nearly so important to him or to his classmates. At least he can be a hero on the ballfield. (Athletic skill is becoming increasingly important for girls as well.) But many learning-disabled (LD) youngsters, whose coordination and athletic prowess are also under par, do not have this relief. They come to expect teasing and rejection no matter where they are.

To see a child socially isolated or rejected hurts caring adults, partly because they sympathize with the child, and partly, perhaps, because it evokes memories of their own painful childhood experiences. While it is neither possible nor even desirable to alleviate all the pain inherent in growing up, obviously we can't merely sit back and watch the child suffer. Unfortunately, however, very little information is available on how to help LD children succeed socially. We are just beginning to understand why these youngsters may relate to others differently and it is only now becoming clear that it may not be possible to treat a learning disability without recognizing the influence of social problems.

The right kind of intervention *can* have an impact. Children's "social quotients" can be raised just as intelligence quotients can be improved when the learning environment changes for the better. Social skills, like academic subjects, must be learned and can be taught. Just as it takes skill to perform well in reading and sports, it takes know-how to behave appropriately. Typically, children with learning differences require careful guidance and teaching at every stage of social development. They don't learn by osmosis. To teach them effectively, adults must first understand the problems which lie within these children as well as those in the environment to which they are responding, and be ready to intervene.

Many youngsters with recognized learning differences in the school years have social problems that persist into adulthood. These problems also persist for parents, teachers, and other caregivers. The pain, embarrassment, and suffering caused by children's unhappiness pervade the lives of everyone involved.

In working with children through the years, I have tried many techniques, some more successfully than others. But as I look back, those children I was able to help the most are those who learned to be successful socially as well as academically. Their parents and teachers were sensitive to their social needs as well as to their reading problems. The understanding and support which accompanied the academic improvement may have had even more lasting and profound effects than the phonics that were drilled. As parents and educators, we have to consider the well-being of the whole child, not only his intellect. To help a child overcome the debilitating effects of his learning disabilities, we must go beyond the three Rs.

NO ONE TO PLAY WITH
PLAY WITH
The Social Side
of Learning
Disabilities

chapter

1

NO ONE
TO PLAY WITH

It was three-fifteen. Mrs. Roberts felt the beginning of a tension headache as she glanced up at the clock. Her daughter would get off the school bus at any moment and then the most difficult part of the day would begin. Janet usually came home from school with a multitude of complaints that had absolutely nothing to do with her learning disability. More often than not they centered on her social problems. Chances were good that she had sat alone on the school bus, been teased at recess, eaten lunch at a table alone, and had a fight with someone—all before three o'clock. Janet's daily recital of social rebuffs was more devastating for Mrs. Roberts than the struggles to learn to read had ever been. Having a child ostracized by her peers was the worst! Mrs. Roberts felt frustrated and helpless.

Janet's learning problems had been recognized by her teacher when she was six. Since then her parents and the school had developed a program to help her. Remedial instruction was provided during the school day, and Janet also came to see me for educational therapy once a week. Now, in sixth grade, her reading was up to grade level and she was even bringing home report cards that her parents could boast about. Why wasn't life serene now that Janet's learning problems had all but disappeared?

The screen door banged and Janet burst into the kitchen in tears. "That damn Bobby! Did his mother call you yet?

Don't believe her. It wasn't my fault. He just won't leave me alone." The words tumbled out, incoherent and unclear. Mrs. Roberts felt her heart sink, but she waited calmly until Janet wound down. This was a familiar scene, typical of the daily routine. There were times when Mrs. Roberts wished there were someone else to greet Janet when she came home reciting her litany of woes. Janet seemed so incapable of coping with life and solving her own problems! At eleven years old, she seemed more like seven or eight.

After milk and cookies and a few words of reassurance from her mother, Janet calmed down. It was a lovely spring afternoon and her mother suggested that she forget her troubles and go out to play. "But I have no one to play with," came the forlorn response. Mrs. Roberts couldn't argue; she knew it was true.

Many of the children who struggle with learning problems in school eventually do find ways to handle their school subjects successfully. Like Janet, these youngsters have compensated for their learning problems, but they remain socially disadvantaged.

Perhaps because children with learning differences look so much like everyone else, it is hard to remember that their problems extend beyond the classroom. Relatives and friends assume that children can leave their academic deficiencies in school and act appropriately after three o'clock but, in many instances, the same characteristics that lead to difficulties in reading and math are responsible for their social ineptitude.

It is well known, for example, that LD youngsters tend to be less mature—in their language, in the quality of their thinking, and even in their physical development. Their social adjustment often reflects this general immaturity. These are the children who seem, like Janet, "eleven going on eight," or who at eighteen are just becoming "typical teenagers."

When Freddy's parents came to see me, they complained that he was having a hard time growing up and the whole family was suffering because of it. Freddy had always seemed babyish at home and now he was finding it hard to keep up with his classmates. He was, his father moaned, "all elbows and fumbles" on the ballfield. Freddy was inevitably the last one picked for a team at recess and he sometimes wasn't chosen at all unless an insistent teacher intervened.

Recently, Freddy had begun to make excuses for staying indoors after school. He would tell his mother that he had "tons of homework" or that he was "coming down with a bad sore throat." Freddy spent most of his free time glued to the TV or provoking his little brother. He was telling lies at home in order to avoid neighborhood activities, and nothing seemed to interest him. His parents watched helplessly as he withdrew further and further into his shell.

Freddy sounded like a clinically depressed adult, the kind who is so unhappy he is unable to function. It is only recently that we have come to realize that children, too, can be depressed. But unlike Freddy, most children manifest their symptoms quite differently from adults. I have seen many LD children whose hyperactivity is really a way of masking their sadness. They fend off the blues by keeping excessively busy. Other youngsters, depressed about their learning disabilities, may eat excessively or have sleep disturbances. They are the night prowlers, too troubled to sleep.

When I saw Freddy, his clothes were a mess, his face and fingernails looked dirty, and he hadn't even bothered to comb his hair. At ten, Freddy seemed very different from other boys his age. He was certainly less mature, and was obviously unhappy. It was as if he had become resigned to his isolation and had even stopped trying to keep up.

There is no easy formula for bringing immature children like Freddy and Janet up to age level. However, there are several ways parents can help them through these growing years. One good approach to the immature child or "late bloomer" is to give him a "gift of time," whenever that is possible. By this I mean that you should try not to compare him with other children his chronological age. It is often helpful to pretend to yourself that a child is really two or three years younger than his birthday indicates. That way, he may look more in step and even seem to be doing the right thing at the right time.

It may sound contradictory, but independence needs to be encouraged for immature children too. When a child seems young for his age and lacks confidence, it is all too easy for parents to foster dependence, especially because the child may be more than willing to go along with it. Freddy's mother used to lay out his clothes for him every night with no objections from her son. He and his mother seemed to have a silent agreement that he would remain a baby. Actually, I began to wonder whether Freddy's dependence served a purpose for his mother too. Her husband traveled on business a great deal and perhaps she wanted to feel needed. When I see parents almost encouraging a child's dependence on them, I look for the gratification it may bring to both parties. There is often a "silent pact" to keep the situation the way it is.

I tried to help Freddy's parents see that his nonexistent social life was related to his unhappiness as well as to his immaturity. His teacher had told me that the other children considered him the baby of the class and wanted nothing to do with him. At that point, his parents and I decided we had better try to do something to help Freddy—in a hurry. For the first time, his parents understood that they could, without concern, encourage him to play with boys in the neighborhood who were younger than he and who liked and even admired him. Anything that would help build his self-esteem was important. In addition, his father tried to spend more time with him working on athletic skills. They had frequent catches and batting practices in the park. Gradually Freddy improved until he could finally join some of the children on the ballfield. He no longer ducked the opportunity to play outside, and occasionally even stayed for after-school sports.

At the same time, Freddy's parents decided to help him become more independent of them. His allowance was increased so that he could save for family presents, buy his own school supplies, and get an occasional ice cream cone. At first, Freddy was surprised and quite scared at the prospect of walking to the stores several blocks away. All this freedom was unexpected. "After all," he said a few times, "I'm still only a kid!" His mother probably agreed because she told me she watched at the window the first few times he took off on his own. Eventually, though, Freddy and his parents accepted that he was no longer a baby. By adolescence, he was even holding down a part-time job.

Immaturity doesn't necessarily end, however, with the onset of puberty, particularly for kids with learning differences. Just because a boy is permitted to drive or a girl wears lipstick, it doesn't mean he or she will act grown-up. Sylvia, an eleventh grader, much preferred the friendship of the ninth-grade girls. She wasn't eager to learn to drive and she couldn't picture herself at college, although we had talked about it often. She had not even begun to menstruate yet and her figure hadn't really matured. She looked and felt very different from her classmates.

As I began to understand how Sylvia felt, I discussed it with her parents (with her permission, of course). It seemed obvious that she needed extra time to catch up. Fate stepped in when Sylvia's father was transferred to another community. This meant that she could repeat a year of high school without embarrassment—more for social than academic reasons. The timing was right, and fortunately Sylvia was comfortable in her new school. It may be a good idea to consider a change of school anyway, even if you don't move, just to give your child the time to catch up.

While not all youngsters can or should repeat a grade at this late date, the extra time worked well for Sylvia. When I last heard, she was off to college, a year late, but convinced now that she could make it.

Once you are aware of an LD child's problems of social immaturity, there are some strategies that seem to help. First of all, allowing a youngster to be his social age and play with others who will accept him will *not* slow down his development, as some adults fear. In fact, associating with younger children allows him to practice getting along with others where it's relatively safe.

Secondly, children may go through a period when they aren't getting along too well with peers and may prefer their own company. This is not the time to push them to seek playmates.

Finally, encouraging self-reliance and independence, even though worrisome for parents, should improve the child's confidence and self-esteem. Giving any child responsibility he can handle helps him to feel more grown-up. It may not be easy to give freedom to a child whose judgment you question, but his learning problem should not become the reason to shield him from the world.

Another common trait of many LD youngsters is that they are impulsive and easily distracted. This is what causes them to speak out of turn in the classroom and makes it hard for them to stick with any game for more than five minutes. They get bored and leave the Monopoly board just when the action is getting good—to the annoyance of their companions. Jack was like that. He would entice a friend to play checkers or dominoes but could not stay with it for more than two turns. Jack would then decide that he didn't want to play that "silly game" after all and would suggest something else. Eventually the friend's head would be swimming with the constant change of activities, and that would be the end of the relationship.

While Jack wasn't exactly hyperactive, his restlessness was annoying to everyone. I remember that even in my office I had to change activities every ten minutes or so to keep his interest. Otherwise he'd begin to look around, ready to dart away at the slightest noise or interruption. And if he couldn't think of any reason for moving around, he'd suddenly have to "go to the bathroom—badly."

Some LD children seem prone to the opposite kind of behavior. Sally Ryan tended to persevere too long, staying with an activity longer than was appropriate, largely because she couldn't "shift gears." When I gave her an assignment, she stuck with it—forever. This behavior caused real problems in the classroom. When her teacher said, "Put away your spelling books, class, and let's begin the math lesson," Sally and one or two other children were unable to make the switch. Five minutes later, they were still struggling with a spelling word or a comma while the class was immersed in long division. This is called "perseveration" and is well recognized as a symptom of learning disabilities.

By the time she was ten, Alice, a classmate of Sally's, was known as "The Mouth" to one and all. She never seemed to stop talking. Her incessant prattle might have seemed cute and disarming when she was tiny, but it no longer ingratiated her with friends or family. As she grew older, Alice's peers began to resent her need to be in the verbal spotlight as well as her lack of tact. She would, for example, tell a joke and then retell it again and again, talking desperately to hold her audience. She also insulted people—not deliberately, but because she seemed unaware of how she sounded.

Alice never seemed to notice that people's expressions would change as she talked on and on. She didn't recognize the signs of boredom, disinterest, or even annoyance in her listeners. By the end of sixth grade, she complained to me that she had very few dates after school with other children and was usually excluded from their parties. She felt hurt and angry at the rejections but couldn't imagine why she was so unpopular. One day she burst into tears in my office, sobbing, "Ann came to my party. How come she didn't ask me to hers? What a louse!"

Children who are insensitive to the reactions of others can frequently embarrass themselves and anyone in their path. Like Alice, they don't watch what they say and seem to suffer from "foot-in-mouth disease." Then it becomes a vicious circle. Because they have no friends to be with, they have no opportunity to learn from others. It's hard to develop social savvy when you're all by yourself!

Alice was fortunate, though, to have a trusting and close

relationship with her mother. Realizing how lonely the child was, Mrs. Benson decided that she had to intervene. Though she felt uncomfortable about doing it without telling her daughter, she phoned Beth, Alice's most recent friend, and asked to meet with her one afternoon. Over an ice cream soda, they discussed Alice's problems very openly. Mrs. Benson said she thought she could understand why Beth and the other girls had dropped her daughter, and she asked for Beth's help.

The next afternoon, Beth and two or three other girls came to Alice's door and asked if they could talk with her. Alice must have been bewildered, but she invited them in. This was the beginning of a two-hour rap session during which the girls confronted Alice with the reasons for her unpopularity. She was in tears, but she listened and apparently *really heard*. At the end of their visit, the girls assured Alice that they wanted to include her again in their group and would do all they could to help her overcome her problems. For the first time, they understood what it felt like to be Alice.

When Mrs. Benson finished her story, I had gooseflesh. This was the most unusual resolution of a problem I had heard. While you could take such direct action only under special circumstances, there probably could be variations on the theme in other situations. For example, when a child has no one to play with and is socially isolated, the first and perhaps most difficult job parents have is to back away and take a long, hard look. What is the child really like? Is he immature and incompetent like Freddy? Does he persevere unreasonably like Sally? Or, as with Alice, do impulsiveness and incessant talking drive people away?

Before it is possible to work out useful techniques of helping, it is important to pinpoint what needs to be changed or modified, the way Alice's mother did. While not everyone is as tuned in and determined a mother, most parents have the capacity to help. This may be hard to do alone, but someone outside the family, perhaps a teacher or friend, can sometimes act as a sounding board when there is trouble.

It might be necessary for someone to interpret a child's actions to him in a way that clearly shows the consequences of what he does. A youngster who lacks perception may need explicit explanations and repeated illustrations before offensive habits can be eliminated. Even then, he may have to be reminded each time he reverts to his old ways. I met a mother whose signal to her daughter was the word *pocket.* It was said whenever the girl was flailing her arms about or being too "touchy" with her hands.

Once social disabilities are identified, there is one key word that should be applied to any strategies that will be tried. That word is *support.* More than other children, the youngster with learning problems lives in an unsteady world. Until he can fend for himself, he needs to learn from the adults in his life and feel he can count on them.

I particularly remember a young mother who told me of a painful encounter that aroused all her supportive instincts. She was taking her three-year-old daughter and five-year-old son to the local school carnival one Saturday. At the penny-toss booth, she met a member of the local LD study group to which she belonged and where she had discussed her son's problems. The co-member suddenly descended upon her like a large bird, asking in stentorian tones, "And which one is your *difficult* child?" Both little ones looked up at their mother while she searched for a rational answer. The best she could do was to respond feebly, "I have no difficult child," as she quickly herded the children off to the next booth. She told me later she wished she had drawn herself up tall and replied, "I have no difficult child. I have a child with a difficulty."

Some adults seem to forget that children have ears—and brains. They talk about them as though they weren't there, making comments that hurt. Children unable to defend themselves need the protection of adults who know better. If a parent is reluctant to make an issue of an inappropriate remark on the spot, he certainly should discuss it with his child at a later time. A comment such as "Aunt Belle hurt your feelings, I know. She probably wasn't thinking at the time, but she had no right to say that," will help. It lets a child know that at least you understand how he feels, and also conveys the message that one should think before speaking. With an older child, further discussion in more depth may be required. I have found that tactless comments tend to fester in children's minds unless they are dealt with.

Most children understand the feelings of others before they understand their thoughts and intentions. By seven or eight, they can even imitate facial expressions and pretend to be sad, happy, fearful, or angry. This skill indicates that the child is accurately perceiving and feeling with others. However, for the LD child with perceptual problems, reading faces may be as difficult as reading numbers or words on a page. If a child misperceives *felt* for *left* and reads *wow* for *mom,* or *19* for *61,* it is not surprising that he would misinterpret social signals too. It is well documented that the LD youngster frequently does not get the same cues as others from his environment. He may not recognize what most of us would perceive as clear signals to stop talking or change the subject. He cannot interpret the meaning or significance of behavior—and misreads the non-verbal cues and body language that communicate so much to most people. This inability may persist for years. There are adults as well as children who seem totally oblivious to the annoyance or even antipathy they are evoking in a social situation because of their inadequate or inaccurate perception—and the lack of empathy that often follows.

A child's use of language also has a great deal to do with his social acceptance. If a youngster is immature in his ability to process words and information, he probably won't understand the idiomatic expressions which are so much a part of daily conversation. Louis, a child I worked with, would miss the thread of many conversations because he interpreted every word literally, if he understood it at all. Then he made his ignorance even more apparent by constantly interrupting the speaker, saying, "What do you mean? I don't get it."

Needless to say, this did not get him approval from those around him. He also failed to laugh at the punch line of a joke, or only managed to chime in after the others' laughter had died down.

Louis was also quite concrete and literal in his thinking. He had trouble handling abstract concepts and was equally unprepared to handle social complexities as they arose. He is the child who when asked how he "found school" one year, replied, "By walking down the street with my mom." And when his mother said she knew that he hit his little sister because she had "eyes in back of [her] head," Louis tiptoed into her room that night to check.

It is customary for most of us to sprinkle our verbal communication with idioms and figures of speech, assuming that we will be understood, at least by those in our own culture. However, parents of children who take everything literally cannot take even ordinary language for granted. They have to be aware that their youngsters process information differently and may be unable to make the logical leaps we expect. When you talk to such a child, imagine that you are speaking to a person from another country, exposed to the language for the first time. Then you will become conscious of figurative expressions and words you are using somewhat differently from their literal meaning.

Parents should also encourage their LD children to ask questions when they don't understand. Unfortunately, this is infrequently done. Too often, because children are made to feel ashamed of what they don't know, they learn to feign understanding. Perhaps, too, their parents are too harried to listen carefully to the signals the youngsters are giving.

Finally, children with learning differences tend to be erratic in their behavior as well as in learning. Their social skills do not develop any more uniformly than their multiplication tables. One day they know 3 × 4, and the next day claim they never saw it before. Similarly, on alternate days they can be unpredictable: irritable or pleasant, attentive or distractible, forgetful or on the ball. When a child suddenly forgets how to play a game he knew the week before or doesn't want to play when his friend does, it can be unsettling and hard to understand. Children want to know that they can count on someone, at least most of the time. No one likes a friend who is both unreliable and unpredictable.

Children with these kinds of behavior patterns have a hard time getting along. Earl, my favorite pessimist, invariably came to our sessions with a gloomy face and a sad tale. "This was the worst day of my life," he'd announce. When I asked him what went wrong, it might have been something as minor as having lost his pencil first thing in the morning. Somehow, he never regained his equilibrium after that minor upset and his day became a disaster. His classmates were well aware of his learning problems and his vulnerability. They teased him about his crying over the lost pencil or a test he failed.

Earl's crankiness at school certainly affected his social life too. He became the original "wet blanket" who could spoil any outing, even a picnic, by complaining about everything —from soup to ants. Eventually, Earl found that he had no one to complain to but his rather unsympathetic family and he was even more unhappy about that.

When Earl was in fifth grade, his parents came to see me about his problems. They kept insisting that his poor school-work was at the root of his unhappiness and irritability and, as it turned out, they were right. As I worked with Earl, I noticed that his optimism increased in direct proportion to his improving grades and confidence in himself.

The social difficulties of some children seem to be directly correlated with their school failure and don't persist once they do better in school. Unlike those of other children with social misperceptions who continue to be misfits even after they can read, Earl's self-esteem and personality improved as his grades did. The time even came when we could laugh about his gripes.

One day, Earl even had the awareness to say to me with

a grin, "I sure do complain a lot, don't I?" We shook hands on that and talked about how his learning problems had spilled over to affect his social life. The kids in his class knew he had reading problems and never let him forget it. No wonder he was so irritable; there was no place where he could be a success. His pain touched me deeply when he said, "There is crying inside me all the time." I could have wept too. As his skills improved, Earl seemed to be able to take life a little more lightly. His classmates must have noticed the change, too, because one day he appeared for his lesson trailed by a friend.

A temper out of control can be grounds for divorce between kids, and LD children are frequently under the kinds of stress that may trigger flare-ups of anger. Mike was a particularly "hot-under-the-collar" kind of boy who was quick to explode. His parents noticed that this was especially true on school days. In trying to handle this with Mike, it occurred to me that it probably took him a couple of hours to recover from the humiliation and frustration he had suffered in the classroom during the day. I helped his parents see this and suggested that Mike go straight home from school to unwind before going out to play. This strategy helped for a while, but one day on his way home, Mike was lured by the prospect of trying out the shiny new bicycle of a neighborhood friend. Fifteen minutes later, when the other boy, Bob, insisted that he get off, Mike "didn't hear him," and when Bob finally pushed him off the bike, Mike stomped on its spokes, damaging them beyond repair.

Mike's grades had been getting better as we worked on his learning disabilities but his temper was as bad as ever. He seemed compelled to ruin things for himself as well as for his family. The current crisis would be expensive as well as frustrating, but it was only one more situation in which Mike overreacted. Any little thing seemed to upset him. His temper was like a time bomb, primed to go off; just a dirty look or an unkind word could trigger an explosion. Although he was too old to be so out of control, his impulsiveness and his irritability made him particularly vulnerable. He lived with hurt feelings and the expectation of rejection.

When Mike's parents called that evening to tell me about the bicycle incident, I mentioned that impulsive youngsters like Mike can often benefit from the techniques developed by proponents of behavior modification. The experts say that it is best to start by identifying and isolating *one* undesirable trait that needs to be changed. For Mike, the obvious one was his temper. I met with Mike's parents to formulate a plan. Then, armed with some ideas, they went home to discuss them with Mike.

First, Mike's parents told him how frustrated they were and how much they wanted to help. For a variety of reasons, Mike had not seen his parents as being "in his corner" before. Previously, family discussions had included his older brother and sister and Mike had always felt humiliated in their presence. They always seemed so perfect and he seemed always to be in trouble.

In private, Mike admitted to his parents that he was just as unhappy about his temper as they were. At times his outbursts even frightened *him.* He felt, though, that no incident was ever his fault; it was always the other guy who set him off. Instead of arguing with Mike this time, his parents went along with his view. "O.K., perhaps you are right, Mike, and the bike incident wasn't entirely your doing. But how else could you have handled it?"

Mike was unable to see any alternative since, after all, Bob had pushed *him.* Mike's parents didn't scold or argue when they heard this. Instead, they merely enacted a little dramatic sketch for Mike. While he watched, his father played Mike and his mother was Bob. Mike's dad showed that the alternative to stomping on the bicycle wheel could have been strong words assertively spoken. These would have been almost as powerful and might have caused far fewer problems.

Mike was amused and impressed by his parents' dramatic

effort, and he did get the point. His temper, in this instance and others they "played out," began to seem ridiculous, even to him. Now he was willing to try to change and get hold of himself. His parents, after we discussed trying to motivate their son, came up with a suitable reward for his controlling his anger. They promised him a popular new record for his stereo if he could keep out of fights for an entire week.

With a younger child, we might have drawn up a chart on which the child could check each successful day—or leave the space blank if he had a fight. Mike agreed to report to his mother or father each day and he used a small spiral notebook to keep track of how things went.

Mike told me that the first week was extremely hard but, at the end, he was amazed that he could go seven days without a fight. Mike got his record and his parents offered another reward for the following week. It's hard to achieve self-discipline in just two weeks' time, though, and Mike "blew it" that week. With encouragement from his parents and from me, he tried again and the third week went well.

After a while, Mike began to control his temper more easily and to deal with his anger in a more mature way. At first, his parents and siblings bore some of the brunt at home since he seemed to have to explode somewhere, but when he finally found a single good friend, the situation at home also eased up. Mike and his new pal used to argue a lot but somehow they remained close most of the time. Controlling his temper was only one of the antisocial kinds of behavior Mike needed to change, but that was the one that had gotten him into the most trouble and therefore was the top priority.

Many youngsters with learning problems have trouble controlling their tempers and their fists, and thereby alienate precisely those children they would love to call their friends. Even if they don't make a habit of fighting physically, they seem to have trouble holding on to friends. Sometimes LD children are unusually bossy, perhaps because they need to feel powerful somewhere, since they cannot in school. Sometimes they hang on too tightly to their friends for fear of losing what they have.

Francine was a child with this kind of problem and the pattern of her friendships was fairly predictable. When she was little, she had played with a next-door neighbor, a younger, rather passive child who would allow Francine to take over in their relationship. When other neighborhood children began to join them, Francine was no longer in control. Her parents told me she would become irritable and have temper tantrums when she didn't get her way.

Eventually, the child next door stayed away and this experience became the first in a series of friendships won and lost. Francine would bring home a new "best friend," and for a few weeks the two would be inseparable. Francine's face would glow as she extolled every virtue of her new-found companion. Then, gradually, there would be a subtle shift in attitude. A criticism or two would creep into Francine's conversation and complaints began to outweigh the praise. Most of the difficulties stemmed from her inability to share her friend with other children and her need to be in charge of their play.

The more the friend pulled away, the more possessive Francine became. "I have to be your only friend," was clearly her attitude. The other child undoubtedly felt smothered and enveloped until she finally severed the alliance altogether. By the end of each relationship, Francine had usually managed to create another enemy for herself. In addition to her learning differences, her social world was populated with those she "hated."

As Francine and I began to talk about those she had alienated, I tried to get her to see the common pattern in each relationship. Francine was angry when I suggested that perhaps she had something to do with her social problems. "How could it be my fault when they're so mean to me?" was her reaction. Helping her see her responsibility for one-half of a whole friendship became my primary goal for her when she was twelve. Over the next few years, Francine's parents and I evolved techniques that began to pay off.

One way her parents were able to help Francine was to adopt a stray kitten for her. Pets can do a lot to give a child a feeling of belonging and can build a sense of responsibility. Almost any child can learn to handle a pet of his own if he really wants to. Francine was encouraged to possess her cat instead of her friend. Then, Francine's parents praised her for any socially acceptable behavior. When she was helpful at home, or generous with a friend, her parents noticed—and commented. Gradually, Francine became more aware of how she acted and how people reacted to her.

A Saturday morning art class provided a social experience for her. The small group that met at the teacher's house was easier for Francine than an intense one-to-one relationship. She didn't really have much artistic talent, but she liked the teacher who was supportive and encouraging.

Finally, Francine's parents tried to include her more in their social activities. They took her out to dinner and to the movies with their friends and their friends' children. This was not only a maturing experience for Francine, but it also let her see how adults interact and get along. By the time Francine was sixteen, she had begun to understand herself better and had learned to reach out to others in a way that didn't alienate them.

Many parents with LD children will feel an uncomfortable familiarity with the Freddys, Alices, Mikes, and Francines they have been reading about. They will feel, "That's my kid!" While each youngster described had his or her unique social problems, the lack of friends and the isolation make all such children "kissin' cousins." Their social dysfunction has kept them apart and unhappy—at least temporarily. The problems are difficult, even for supportive parents and professionals; far more difficult, in some instances, than their school problems.

Few children improve quickly but there are a few guidelines which may be applied to a majority of children who lack companionship during the school years. First, it may help to remember that *not every child alone is a lonely child.* Some children are by nature quietly creative and prefer their own company much of the time. Perhaps the criterion would be whether the child is alone by choice or necessity. To force a child to go to an activity because a neighbor's kids are going may not be best for him. Perhaps this is another time to stand back and take an objective view. Does he really need to be off and running, or would a quiet afternoon at home do just as well? So often LD children are exhausted when they get home from school because they have expended all their energy just getting through the day. They may need to recoup their strength before facing yet another challenge.

Children with a history of problems in school are usually more insecure than their peers. They are burdened with the knowledge that it is harder for them to learn than it is for others. They may have acquired doubts along the way about their own competence and worth. When parents try to make them fit into the mold of children their age, everyone is bound to be disappointed. *Acceptance* is the most difficult thing to achieve, but it is probably the most crucial gift parents can give a child with learning problems. Only when he feels accepted *with his differences* can he begin to gain inner strength and the courage to persevere.

One way to foster acceptance from peers is to find an area in which a child has special ability. A girl who doesn't like volleyball may do nicely in tap shoes. I knew a boy who began collecting rocks at camp and wound up as an assistant to the naturalist at the local museum. He gained a lot of status with his peers and no one even remembered that he had not made Little League.

When a child begs to try something new in September— like woodworking or gymnastics—many parents insist that he stick with the class until June. Children have suffered through an entire series of lessons which they hate and for which they lack talent just because of the puritanical myth "You must finish what you start." Somehow, we just can't accept the idea that a child can change his mind or become discouraged. For example, the youngster with learning problems may think he wants to try woodworking but then find that he can't handle the tools.

When it becomes clear to you, as a parent, that a new interest or activity has become just one more defeat for the child, you probably ought to let him stop. This may be one more instance where we have to treat the LD child with a little extra sensitivity. I'd suggest letting him taste and try without requiring a long-term commitment. It may take several false starts before he becomes excited by an activity or prospective hobby, but it is usually worth the search—both for the sense of achievement and the social experience.

It is obvious that successful children attract more praise —and need it less—than those who constantly live with failure and frustration. Along with acceptance, *compliments and positive feedback, when honestly given, are like vitamins that encourage growth and self-confidence.* We should probably dispense them more freely than we do, especially to LD children.

While waiting for children to grow up and overcome their social disabilities, it might be a good idea to take a look at their peer group through their eyes. One particularly nonconformist mother I knew encouraged all her children to be individualistic. Harold, though, was different enough from the rest because of his learning problems. He didn't need to be a practicing nonconformist too. Besides, he wanted desperately to "belong" to the gang.

Harold's mother, insensitive to the dress code of the day, had been giving Harold his brother's hand-me-downs. The clothes were no longer in style and were "babyish." While the new jeans and shirts I encouraged her to buy didn't accomplish miracles, Harold certainly felt more "in." Harold's mother had put aside her own tastes in order to help her son look more like the rest of the group.

At some point, most parents decide to give in to the latest fads, particularly at the stage of development when conformity to the peer group seems to matter most. This does not mean, necessarily, that a child will grow up always following the crowd, but conformity may be important for a while—particularly for a child with learning difficulties who is having trouble finding his place among his contemporaries.

The socially competent youngster usually is comfortable enough to extend himself fully and freely into the world. He isn't afraid to be himself and he isn't ashamed to be wrong. While not every child with learning problems experiences social problems, the child who does not do well socially needs special understanding—both of the sort of person he is and of the sort of world in which he lives.

chapter
2

LOOKING BACK: THE BEGINNINGS

Unless there are very unusual circumstances, social problems don't suddenly start when children are nine or ten years old. Sometimes the beginnings can be traced back to a child's earliest years—long before his learning disabilities are recognized. Parents of teenagers with learning problems and/or social disabilities often claim they knew something was wrong almost from the start. They may describe a baby like Buddy, so different from his friendly, easygoing older brother who did everything "according to the book." When Buddy was born, his parents expected more of the same. After all, hadn't they learned on their first child? The second boy ought to be even easier.

Buddy was a surprise—and a disappointment—even in infancy. He cried a great deal, especially at night, and pushed his mother away when she most felt like cuddling him. "It was hard to feel loving toward this baby who never seemed to love us back," Mrs. O'Hara recalled years later. Those early days were so filled with frustration and bewilderment, it was almost a relief when Buddy's learning problems were diagnosed in kindergarten and seemed to provide an explanation for his behavior.

We are just beginning to understand that social interaction starts very early in the human life cycle, actually at the time of birth. Many children, later found to have learning problems, seem to begin their lives with unexpected or inappropriate responses to their first social contacts. They may be fussy, cranky infants or restless sleepers or finicky eaters who keep their parents busy twenty-four hours a day. While such behavior does not necessarily predict either learning differences or social maladjustment, these first interactions can create tension and anxiety for parents and signify the beginning of a difficult relationship.

Psychiatrists Chess and Thomas talk about several patterns of temperament in newborn children which may indicate they are extra-sensitive to their surroundings and perhaps more susceptible to social problems as they mature. When parents and caring adults are able to identify these patterns, they may tune in better to the baby's needs and personality. Most psychologists agree with Chess and Thomas that appropriate handling can "minimize or even eliminate the development of behavior disorders."* I would add to this the possibility that future school problems will also be minimized with good management in the early years.

Tommy was one of the children whose infancy foreshadowed trouble. Years later, his parents remembered that the nurse in the hospital had told them their husky two-day-old son was having a hard time settling down in the nursery. Mrs. Potter sighed deeply when she told me this, saying, "I guess I knew he was going to be a handful even before he was born. He never stopped kicking inside me."

The Potters' problems escalated when they brought Tommy home. He was a light, fitful sleeper and a poor eater who seemed to vomit even more than he ate. He was easily startled by moderately loud noises, cried constantly with colicky distress, and seemed inconsolably miserable much of the time. In short, he was an exhausted, unhappy baby, with parents to match.

At eighteen months, Tommy raced rather than toddled. A trip to the supermarket became a major production requiring

*Thomas, A. and Chess, S., *Temperament and Development*. New York: Brunner-Mazel, 1977, p. 62.

much advance planning and at least one other adult to chase Tommy through the aisles. After too many frustrating trips, Mrs. Potter finally gave up and left Tommy with his father while she did her errands alone. In fact, Tommy was rarely taken anywhere and thus was deprived of some of the early learning experiences most children have.

When the Potters discussed Tommy's behavior with their family doctor, he was sympathetic. He told them that most youngsters like Tommy do calm down eventually. Unless they are sick, their early irritability and restlessness may be caused by immaturity or a response to something going on in the family. Growth is rarely a smooth, unbroken thread between infancy and adulthood. Some children, though, do continue to be hyperactive. "It may seem strange," the doctor told them, "but sometimes extremely active children receive so much attention and stimulation that they become even more so."

Before Tommy's problems got any worse, the doctor urged the Potters to take preventive measures. To understand the family better, he asked Mr. and Mrs. Potter about their own backgrounds. He was not too surprised to learn that Tommy's mother had always been considered "hyper" by her family. As an adult, she had channeled a great deal of energy into keeping her family well-functioning. She was up early in the morning and worked late most nights. Since Tommy was restless himself, he often kept her company as she raced around the house. She rarely rocked him or held him quietly. In short, she presented a perfect model of how to grow up hyperactive. Tommy was getting maternal attention by keeping pace with his busy mom.

It was becoming apparent, though, that Tommy was not evoking warm or loving reactions from his parents. Quite the contrary, they were frustrated and impatient with him. Their physician suggested ways to slow Tommy down a bit and get rid of some of his excess energy—lots of pull toys, banging and hammering sets, and soft, fluffy "sit-upons." He suggested that Mrs. Potter herself take things easier, reserve time to sit quietly with her child, and strive for tranquil communication and pleasure.

Discipline, usually a difficult area for parents of active children, had to be consistent and firm for Tommy. "No" had to mean "no" and be clearly understood, but not overused. Sometimes parents tend to say "don't" too quickly with the hard-to-manage child. They automatically assume that trouble is brewing. In fact, some children hear "no" or "don't" so often that the words become meaningless. There is a possibly apocryphal anecdote of a three-year-old whose proud grandmother introduced her to a neighbor. When asked her name, the little girl replied, "Nancy." "Nancy what?" was the next question. "Nancy Don't," came the prompt reply.

Support in these kinds of situations can come from many sources. For the Potters, it was their pediatrician who stayed in touch with the family and gave them the courage to stick to their guns when they might have wavered. The more consistent discipline and scheduling eventually helped the family live more comfortably with Tommy's frenetic pace. The Potters were also better able to admit that Tommy's personality *was* difficult and not blame themselves for getting annoyed with him.

Fortunately for parents and the world at large, not all children with difficult temperaments are as active as Tommy —or as exhausting. Patsy, a premature baby, stayed in the hospital for three weeks, until she weighed enough to go home to join her three older siblings in an active household. She was welcomed as though she were a new doll for her sisters to play with.

Patsy was an easygoing baby who seldom fussed and demanded little. Even in the first year, though, her mother felt some nagging concern when she compared her baby's development with that of her other children. Patsy just wasn't as alert as the others had been. At first, she reassured herself that Patsy had been premature, and that often means slower development. Then, too, theirs was a noisy, bustling household. It was easy to overlook a baby who was so easy and placid. Mrs. Teal's last thought was, perhaps, a guilty one. Since Patsy demanded little, she was left alone a good deal. Mrs. Teal decided that, in spite of the demands of the other children, she would try to set aside time to play with her baby and introduce her to new sights and sounds. Her efforts were only partially successful, though, in spite of her good intentions.

By the time she was ten months old, Patsy was gradually becoming more a part of the household, but no one except family members could hold her or care for her. She would be cheerful enough while seated in her high chair at the dinner table, but when a stranger appeared, she cried hysterically. An indulgent grandmother was the only baby sitter Patsy would tolerate.

When the Teals questioned experts about Patsy's shyness and fear of strangers, they were reassured that nothing was wrong. This was just a "typical stage" in development which she would soon outgrow. "Wait until she's a toddler; you'll be running after her," they said. But this was not the case. By the age of two, though she no longer screamed at the sight of strangers, Patsy withdrew more and more. She would sit quietly in her rocker, sucking her thumb, clutching her worn, old blanket, looking sad. Mrs. Teal admitted that she often became impatient with Patsy's passivity and her slowness to learn. Patsy was a late talker, speaking only a few words at an age when many children were beginning to speak in sentences. It bothered Mrs. Teal that her daughter wouldn't even try anything new. She seemed all too willing to sit and let life go on around her.

Mrs. Teal enrolled Patsy in nursery school when she was three, hoping to jolt her out of her inertia and further her language development. Patsy did not want to leave the safety of her home for nursery school, though, and she had a hard time separating from her mother. It took her the better part of the semester to leave her mother's side. Even then, she was a loner, playing by herself in the doll corner. The teachers and pediatrician felt it was best to leave her alone and again the Teals heard, "That's O.K. She'll talk and join the group when she's ready." So no one made an effort to see that either of these things happened. Years later, Patsy's parents realized that perhaps because Patsy hadn't made waves, she had been shortchanged. They felt their lack of awareness and attention to Patsy may have contributed to her problems.

Nevertheless, the Teals were surely not responsible for Patsy's learning disabilities. In fact, there was a history of mild learning problems on both sides of the family. I talked with the Teals about the many youngsters with learning disabilities who don't seem to learn merely by living. These are the children who need even more stimulation—not less —than others.

Delayed speech is not only a common forerunner of learning differences, but a deterrent to social development as well. Children who can't communicate easily usually can't play as well with peers. They tend to stand on the sidelines observing what others are doing, or they play silently alone.

Since children learn language by imitation and practice, youngsters like Patsy need extra attention and exposure to the spoken word. Bringing an infant into the middle of family activities and speaking to him about events he may not yet even understand form the basis of language.

Another way of stimulating toddlers is to let them see other children. Patsy might have been less shy at nursery school if she had had prior experience with young children. Two or three toddlers in a sandbox can provide role models, even at such an early age.

Enrolling Patsy in nursery school was a good idea, but she probably should have been gently urged to participate with the group. She was not growing when she was alone in the doll corner; she was not learning to share and cooperate. These are social skills that young children acquire by interacting with others.

Not all frustrating or hard-to-live-with babies are like the two youngsters mentioned here. Each child is unique in temperament and response to the world. Patsy and Tommy are only two of the many LD children I have known who seemed to have had social difficulties right from the start. They didn't quite fit the patterns described in baby books; nor did they fulfill their parents' expectations.

All children are born with their own personalities and temperaments which are apparent within the first few hours of life. While no conclusions can be drawn about later development, some children's social responses at any age may be signposts saying, "Watch out! Trouble ahead." Strained relationships may form between parent and baby. Without intervention, these may persist and affect a child's future adjustment.

We take it for granted that no one can resist a baby, but tired, overworked parents of difficult children may find little that is attractive about their offspring. They may be disappointed and frustrated—and have no one to turn to for help with a child they can't relate to or don't understand. Without a family network of grandparents and relatives nearby, many modern parents are more alone with their children than ever before in history.

In the past few years, in response to the need of parents for the companionship and the advice of other parents, "walk-in" centers have opened in many communities. People bring their infants or toddlers to the centers to learn more about the art of parenting and about how to enjoy their children. There is usually an early childhood specialist who sets an example for inexperienced mothers and fathers. Handling techniques, play activities, and learning situations are demonstrated and discussed. It is assumed that parents will translate what they learn and be more competent with their youngsters.

A child isn't a baby very long. At some time during the toddler stage, he usually becomes aware that there are others like him all over the playground or park. These first social experiences with other children mean leaving the bosom of his family, if only to play a few feet away from the mother.

Watching toddlers at play, it is easy to spot the aggressive bully who terrorizes the other children and the watchful soul who never leaves his mother. In this informal setting, social problems become evident. Some may be related to a youngster's delayed language development, short attention span, or immaturity. These are also signposts of learning disabilities once the child gets to school. Since there are no college degrees offered in parenting, parents must rely on their intuition when they make judgments about their child's development. I find that parental intuition is usually valid. Though each child has his own timetable, if you spot a consistent pattern of social difficulties, even at a very early age, do not ignore it or pretend it doesn't exist. A child with learning differences that impede social growth needs the love and attention all toddlers need—and more. He may need a stimulating environment to build on his strengths and encourage his overall development.

Today, with more women in the work force, there is an increasing trend toward day care and nursery school for toddlers. Consequently, socialization is forced at an earlier age than it used to be when mother and grandmother were around all the time. With more little ones in early childhood programs, social differences can often be spotted and worked with by perceptive, alert teachers. Rather than waiting to identify children with learning disabilities until the second or third grade, a lot of suffering can be avoided by an early response to striking social inadequacy and/or apparent learning problems.

When the need is indicated, a pediatrician, psychologist, or learning specialist can do a preliminary screening on a child to provide parents with diagnostic information. For the child with very special needs, a therapeutic nursery may be recommended. This is a setting in which specially trained therapist/teachers work on the children's problems in small groups and teach them social skills. One little boy I have worked with was expelled from Head Start because he was hyperactive and aggressive but did beautifully in the therapeutic nursery where the staff helped him develop self-control and the beginning of cooperation.

Early social interaction has undisputed value for personality development, but it also stimulates intellectual growth. How a youngster relates to others and how they feel about him profoundly affects his self-image, his motivation to learn, and his future attitude toward school. This is reason enough not to ignore problems in the early years. Deliberate, formal teaching is only part of the wider spectrum of experiences that contribute to a young child's social development. Informed, involved parents are a young child's most special resource.

GETTING ALONG
IN THE FAMILY

Taking care of a child who does not respond as other children do, and who makes parents feel they never get through to him verbally or emotionally is a very hard load to carry, for love is ordinarily a reciprocal experience. Trying to maintain some semblance of stability in the home with a child who overreacts to practically everything, who has temper tantrums on almost no provocation, who seems to gravitate to the most undesirable companions, or who cannot be made to understand why the reins must be tighter on him than on more normal children would try anyone's patience.*

Youngsters learn and practice their first social skills within the family. When appropriate behavior is difficult for them, family life can become chaotic and relationships may be strained to the breaking point. Then, not only is the LD child the loneliest person in the neighborhood, he is likely to have problems with his family as well.

Danny was one such youngster. He explained to me, "I always get into trouble at home because I do bad things."

"Like what?" I inquired.

"Like just about everything," came the reply.

Danny was an attractive but usually sad nine-year-old who

*Anderson, C.M., *Society Pays.* New York: Walker & Co., 1972, p. 16.

always seemed to be the "odd man out" with his parents and his younger brother. I was trying to understand what went on in his family that made life so difficult for all of them.

When Danny's parents came to my office later that week, they confessed with some embarrassment that Danny *was* hard to live with and his mother frankly admitted she couldn't wait for him to go to summer camp. She needed a rest, she said, from the constant fighting at home. Danny didn't seem to get along with the members of his own family any better than he did with his classmates and his teachers in school. He had always been a difficult child, even as an infant, and never seemed to quite fit into the family. "Maybe if Danny had been born to other parents, he could have managed better," Mrs. Grant sighed.

She went on to say that Danny was an active, demanding and volatile little boy, while she and her husband and Danny's younger brother, Eddie, were more even-tempered and quiet. In short, Danny's personality was even more of a problem to the family than the mild-to-moderate learning difficulties for which I had been seeing him.

Many parents of children with learning differences undoubtedly feel as Danny's mother did. Children like Danny have a hard time handling all the daily interactions with parents, siblings, and other members of the household. Their presence can convert an ordinary activity like dinner into a time of tears and tension.

The pattern was always the same in this particular family. Danny told me he tried hard to sit still at the dinner table, but he never seemed to get past the main course without forfeiting dessert. His father admitted that Danny's inability to sit quietly and his total disregard for any eating utensils other than his fingers irritated him to the breaking point. Try as he would, Mr. Grant found that his patience would come to an abrupt end in the middle of dinner and inevitably Danny would be banished from the table. On his way out, Danny might give his brother a fast kick or a curse, triggering tears and complaints from that quarter. Then his mother would follow Danny out of the room, trying to placate him with the dessert he had already lost. I could just imagine how the battle lines were drawn—angry father and brother against mother and Danny.

"You always give in to him!" Mr. Grant frequently accused his wife.

"Well, he can't help it. You know he has problems," Mrs. Grant would shout in Danny's defense. Then, feeling guilty about her part in all of this, she, too, wound up frustrated and angry at Danny. Sometimes she'd turn on him, shouting, "Why do you have to spoil so many dinners for everyone? Don't you love us at all?" Once she sheepishly confessed to me that she had even accused Danny of "messing up" her marriage by provoking so many fights in the family.

Late into the evening, Danny's parents would argue about what had gone on at the dinner table. And mealtimes were not the only trouble spots in Danny's life at home. The Grants reported that they were just a few of the many unpleasant scenes in the drama entitled "Life with Danny."

Actually, Danny's conflicts with his family began early in the day. On weekdays he'd come down for breakfast in his before-school bad mood, having already picked at least one fight with his brother. Not only was Danny apprehensive about the academic problems that awaited him in the classroom, it also enraged him that Eddie could brush his teeth, make his bed, gather his schoolbooks and be at the table before him. Eddie seemed so perfect that Danny couldn't stand it.

In one respect, though, Danny was fortunate. He had only one "super" brother to contend with. Many children with learning differences have more than one sibling at home to compare themselves to and be frustrated by.

When Danny's parents and I talked about the long list of events they dreaded, family get-togethers were close to the top. Company always seemed to push Danny's "ornery button." He acted rude, noisy, and stand-offish to relatives and friends who hadn't seen him for a while and who couldn't wait to hug him. He usually managed to insult doting aunts and he had even been known to use some choice curse words in his grandparents' presence.

Mrs. Grant couldn't decide whether Danny's "company behavior" was simply attention-getting or was the result of his inability to handle so much excitement at one time. All she knew was that from the moment the doorbell rang, he became impossible. She felt that just because he had learning problems, it shouldn't mean he had the right to be obnoxious and to embarrass the family.

Danny didn't even need a crowd in the house to act up. Any unfamiliar person or change in his normal routine could trigger a scene. Baby sitters were among his favorite targets. Very few of them had survived over the years because Danny was so hard to handle when his parents were out. He could be depended upon to get into fierce battles with his brother or refuse to go to bed on time—in short, to defy all the rules that his mother had spelled out so carefully before she left. The Grants usually returned from an evening out to find a frazzled sitter and a tearful Danny waiting up for them.

Eventually, it seemed more trouble than it was worth to go out, so the Grants usually stayed home—and resented it! When Danny went to summer camp, it provided the only respite for them in the whole year. No wonder they couldn't wait for him to leave! But there was always the worry that camp would send him home, since along with Danny's other problems, he still, at nine, had occasional day- and nighttime "accidents." He also wasn't particularly careful about keeping himself clean. As Mrs. Grant came to feel more comfortable in our relationship, she admitted to me that while she felt sorry for Danny, this aspect of his problems was hardest for her to bear. It offended her sensibilities and she just couldn't seem to control her reaction of anger and disgust. She only hoped that Danny's camp counselor would be more patient.

After years of consulting specialists, the Grants had come to understand that Danny was not necessarily behaving defiantly when he didn't make it to the bathroom in time. The doctors said that in all probability he did not always get the clear signals that other children do. His nervous system was less mature, and his anxiety and continual frustration certainly didn't help the problem.

Danny obviously had his own resentments toward his family. He told me that he felt like he didn't even belong to his parents. Sometimes he wondered if they had really adopted him and weren't telling him the truth. I could imagine that his parents occasionally had similar fantasies, musing about whether there had been a switch in the hospital nursery after all. Otherwise, where had this very different child come from?

The hurt that both Danny and his parents felt was like a contagious illness passing between them. Pain makes people anxious and sometimes even unreasonable. When parents are unable to understand and cope with children's behavior, they are, quite understandably, edgy and off balance.

As I thought about the Grants, it became clear to me that all of them had assumed specific roles that they were stuck with. Danny's brother had been labeled "Super-kid." He could do no wrong in his parents' eyes and, in fact, he usually didn't. Danny, on the other hand, was "the villain," always making trouble. Though she was becoming increasingly angry with him, Mom tended to act as his ally and defender, while his father was forced into the role of the "heavy."

The first thing to work on seemed to be the relationship between Danny and his parents. He needed to feel accepted by them before he could feel good about himself. It isn't easy to overlook a constant stream of misdeeds, but I thought that perhaps the Grants' standards had been too high and unrealistic for Danny. Since no transgression was ever ignored, there was no way he could gain approval. There needed to be more emphasis on the things Danny did right at home. That could be the first step in helping him feel better about himself as a more integral part of the family.

Another of Danny's problems was that he had no activities or interests that took him outside the house. Like many youngsters with learning problems, he didn't make or keep friends easily, and because he had so few pals in the neighborhood, he usually hung around at home with his mom. That was less than ideal for a growing boy who needed active play. His parents and I looked long and hard for an activity for him and we finally came up with swimming at the YMCA. It wasn't too competitive and it wasn't far from home. We hoped the program would provide a good social experience for Danny as well as a chance to succeed at something all his own.

Danny, predictably, was reluctant at first. He had always been afraid to try anything new, probably because he was sure he'd fail. LD youngsters experience so much failure in their lives that they rarely approach anything new with confidence, but Danny's mother insisted and she found a friend's child willing to go to the pool with him.

After a couple of weeks of being pushed to go, Danny admitted that he really was beginning to like swimming. He also found, to his surprise, that he was good at it. Swimming, incidentally, is often a good activity for those children with learning disabilities who have trouble with team sports. They don't have to be quick on their feet and they don't even have to remember in which direction to run.

After a while, Danny's parents were able to handle the company situation more easily too. Relatives and friends were advised not to rush him when they arrived; conversely, Danny was not expected to perform for them. As a result, he began to warm up, particularly to his grandparents, who, in turn, began to appreciate some of his good qualities.

Somehow, the problems of mealtime eventually diminished as well, probably as a result of Danny's maturing and his parents' better understanding of him. Mr. Grant said he realized that Danny really *couldn't* sit through a leisurely meal, particularly one spiked with conversation about his parents' frustrations at their respective offices. So Danny and Eddie were allowed to leave the table without threat of punishment when they were finished eating.

Once Danny was given more freedom to leave the table,

he apparently didn't even use the privilege very often. Because he was more relaxed, he sometimes managed to sit with them for a longer time. Coincidentally, I noticed an increase in his attention span in my office as well—and surely a cheerier personality. Danny was living proof that tension and frustration can tend to make a "hyper" child even more so. Behavior can improve significantly when even a little pressure is removed.

There is little doubt that children with learning disabilities frequently have personality characteristics that make the job of parenting more difficult. Like Danny, they are often irritable, impulsive, and volatile. They may be so hard to handle, in fact, that parents give in to them more than they should. It seems to be easier to do so, but, in fact, by acceding to their every wish, parents may unwittingly be creating unhappy tyrants in the house. As these children grow, so does their domination over the others in the family. This creates resentment from their "subjects" and also sets up a pattern of behavior that spills over to the school and playground. Then the social problems of such children become even greater, since no one wants to play with a "dictator."

In my work with children who present difficult management problems for their families, I find that, even more than the youngsters themselves, it is the parents who need support in order to change relationships at home. Their attitudes need to be clarified and their feelings dealt with. Parents may have to learn that it is not child abuse to say "No" and mean it.

This change in attitude can only take place when parents lose their fear of their children. It may sound strange, but many parents seem more afraid of alienating their children than the other way around. The "special" child in the family may be given whatever he wants in order to keep peace at any price. A recent study has shown that mothers of LD children who have come to accept their children's problems in a friendly, non-hostile way are also comfortable about assuming a firmer, more authoritarian role.

Actually, even though they may protest, youngsters appreciate firmness and control. This is particularly true of LD children whose lives are filled with uncertainties and insecurities. A steady, *consistent,* and well-articulated pattern of expectations from their parents is an important stabilizer for them. How many times I have heard young people say with bravado, "It's my life and I can handle it," when in fact they were scared to death of the prospect. In addition, the poor judgment which often accompanies their learning difference and their lack of social experience may prevent them from appraising realistically just what they are capable of doing.

One twelve-year-old boy, whose parents were going on vacation, could not understand why they wouldn't leave him at home for the week with his dog for companionship. He acknowledged that he might get a bit lonely at times, but he figured that he could watch TV, fix cold cereal for his meals, and call his parents on the telephone (a thousand miles away) if he needed them! His parents' firm "No, Grandmother will stay with you," finally put an end to these grandiose fantasies.

When children have social problems at home it isn't always because they are provocative or creating chaos. They may not be noisy or excitable but, instead, may stay quietly in the background making no waves at all. Their lack of involvement in the family, though, can be just as upsetting as other children's disruptive behavior. Parents and siblings may not know how to relate to these reticent children nor how to bring them into the family circle. Many families, in fact, give up and let those children who are "different" become outsiders.

Susan Thomas is a child who felt like a foreigner in her own home, but instead of making a lot of commotion the way Danny had, she withdrew and tried to stay out of trouble. At nine, she spent most of her free time playing alone in her bedroom to avoid being tormented by her older sister and brother. "Retard" and "Stupid" were their favorite names for her, and they weren't only said in jest. Her siblings knew that Susan was in a special class for children with learning disabilities and they never let her forget it.

When Susan felt picked on, she would run to her room, slam the door, and even break her own toys in frustration. She said there was no way she could fight back. Her sister and brother could easily beat her up, and she was convinced they would. Susan was also afraid to tell her parents because of the threat of more aggression from her siblings if she tattled on them. She was really in a bind.

One day when she was in my office working on a math assignment, Susan burst into tears. After a few minutes, she was able to tell me just how miserable she felt at home. "No one talks to me. They either yell at me or tease. And no one ever wants to be with me—even Mom and Dad. I wish I had a dog to love."

A week or two later, Susan came up with the idea of having her family join us in my office for one session. She and I had talked by ourselves about her problems with her brother and sister but she was afraid to confront them directly without me. When we all met, Susan's siblings were particularly eager to say what had been on their minds too. They talked very openly of their resentment. Her sister said, "What bothers me is that Susan is such a sourpuss. She's not a good sport and she doesn't even try to make friends. She's just not at all sociable."

Her brother added, "Yeah, she just stands there like a lump and she won't even try to learn how to play our games. That's why we can't include her in anything. And most of all, I hate having to explain what's the matter with her to all the kids. They think she's queer."

Her sister let out a sigh. "If only she didn't have learning problems, she wouldn't be so embarrassing."

During this meeting, I realized that Susan did, indeed, make life difficult for her brother and sister. It was apparent that they resented having to be responsible for Susan when their parents weren't home and having to make excuses to their friends for her peculiarities. Maybe they also felt that in some way their friends were blaming them for Susan's behavior. Finally, I knew that they felt guilty that Susan had so many problems and they didn't. While it may seem illogical, a common reaction of siblings is a feeling of guilt for having been born without problems. These feelings are both normal and understandable.

After our meeting, Susan's parents told me they, too, had recognized what a burden Susan had become for their other children. They probably had pushed Susan's brother and sister to assume responsibility for her that was beyond their limits. Mr. and Mrs. Thomas had not been entirely unaware of what Susan had been going through at home, but their philosophy had always been that children should work out their problems for themselves. They deliberately tried to remain neutral and ignore their children's fights. What they had not realized, though, was that in a way, they were actually giving tacit permission for the older ones to make a scapegoat of Susan.

But, of course, Susan also played a part in what was happening. She and I talked about how she avoided confronting her family when they made her angry or unhappy. I suggested that she might even be afraid to be angry. Susan laughed and said, "I used to think that if I got really mad, a monster would eat me up!"

I helped her understand that instead of exposing that "monster," she had kept her feelings inside—supposedly out of reach. However, she was really hurting herself and, at the same time, encouraging her brother and sister to pick on her. Perhaps underneath she felt she deserved it. After years of suffering from learning problems in school and at home, it is only natural that youngsters begin to feel that they can't do anything right. They accept any criticism as justified, even expected.

Having a sibling with a handicap of any kind is almost always a problem for a child. Typically, he feels sorry for the affected brother or sister, but at the same time resents being associated with someone who is so out of step. And that resentment is magnified when the sibling's learning disability constantly gets in the way of normal family functioning. Frequently the angry feelings are bottled up until they finally explode on the one who is the source of all that guilt and embarrassment.

Sibling rivalry is commonplace, even expected in most families, particularly when children are close in age. When one child has a handicap, however, that rivalry may escalate to a destructive level. The LD child may be jealous of his "normal" siblings for whom life is undoubtedly easier, while his brothers and sisters are resentful of the extra attention given the problem child.

Jealousy and resentment between children cannot be wished away, but need to be handled by parents. One important factor is the attitude of parents. If one child is obviously favored, or if the LD child is regarded as a burden, resentment among siblings will be increased. If, on the other hand, the youngster with a problem is a fully accepted and welcome member of the family, the extra attention he requires will probably be more easily tolerated by brothers and sisters.

There are three strategies adults can use when war does break out between children. They can separate the children, overlook their fighting, or intervene. None of these will be appropriate all the time, but each may have its place at one time or another.

No parent likes to see his children at odds with each other, yet experts feel that these conflicts are not necessarily all negative. They teach children patience and forbearance and, in addition, teach them some techniques of winning. It may make sense, though, to separate youngsters who are too aggressive and competitive with each other. Finding different interests fosters more individuality and less competition. It may be more convenient to have all the children in a family on the same swim team, but it will undoubtedly put one child at a disadvantage. Even if the LD child happens to excel, it's still better for him to have the honor all to himself.

"Fair is not always equal" is a good rule to follow. Children may need to go to bed at different times, to do homework in different places, and to be alone with a parent when they need it most. Parents who try to treat all the children the same may only be exacerbating the resentment among them.

Whenever possible, ways should be found for children to feel special. In one family I know, the eldest boy, who happened to have a learning difference, was put to bed at the same time as his younger sisters. He was, admittedly, a handful, so his parents were ready to call it a day at eight o'clock, even though he wasn't. He resented this and took it out on his sisters. When I suggested that he have a few extra minutes to spend with his father at bedtime, he felt privileged and acted accordingly.

It is hard for parents to know when to ignore a battle, particularly if the youngest in the family is in the middle of things. But left alone, most children work things out without killing each other. A parent's interference can escalate a small matter into a conflagration. Judgment plays a big part in determining when to stay out of an argument and when to intervene.

There are times when a child needs protection, as Susan Thomas did. More often than not, it is the LD child who is defenseless. Even younger siblings can provoke and tease him, particularly if they get the response they want—and enough support from parents. It is natural for parents to come to the defense of a younger child, but parents may be coming to the rescue of the wrong party. No child should be allowed to ride roughshod over a brother or sister, regardless of age or status. When this happens, parents have to convey the idea that such behavior is completely unacceptable and impose some strong controls.

The families of Danny and Susan were basically intact, with deep concern for their children and their problems. They had done everything they could to provide the right kind of help to remedy their children's school problems, but were aware that they had been far less effective in solving the problems at home. In fact, at one time or another both the Grants and the Thomases had confessed to me that they were completely caught up in their children's LD problems and felt their other children were being short-changed in terms of parental attention. Mr. Grant thought it might have been better if Danny had been the only child in the family.

I have heard other parents of LD children express this feeling, but actually, there are problems in being an only child too, particularly when the child has a learning disability. Only children are often the recipients of extra attention and certainly a great deal of scrutiny from parents. When that child has a learning difference, he may feel like an insect under the microscope—nothing goes unnoticed. It is quite different from being one of four kids in the family where there's at least a chance of escaping with some flaws undetected. An only child often feels an added responsibility to his parents—after all, they've invested so much in him. But with his learning problems, it may be impossible for him to please them. So it's frustrating for both parents and child.

Diana Harris was the child of professional parents who had chosen to limit their family to one. They were devoted to Diana and had high hopes for her, so it was a crushing blow when her first-grade teacher told the Harrises that Diana was not keeping up with her class. Her parents were amazed, having assumed that Diana was easily as bright as her peers. Since she was their only child, though, they had no basis for comparison.

When I met the family, Mr. and Mrs. Harris were frustrated as well as disappointed. They were obviously feeling, "We have only one child to fulfill our dreams. Why did this have to happen to us?" I sensed that they were really very angry that their daughter could not live up to their expectations. To make matters worse, they felt so guilty about their feelings toward Diana that they had allowed her to dominate the family. Diana was developing into a bossy, demanding little girl who wasn't much fun to live with. It was apparent that the Harrises were suffering along with their daughter, but their disappointment in her was so deep-seated, it was to be immutable for a long time to come.

Eventually, counseling was recommended to help the Harrises deal with their disappointment. They had had too many hopes and dreams for one little girl to fulfill. Diana was burdened and they were angry. They had to allow her to be herself, learning problems and all, and they needed more of a life of their own. Summer camp, sleep-over dates away from home, and adult-only vacations were suggested. All these helped restore some balance in the family.

It is understandable that parents resent a child's learning disability to some extent. Somehow, the image of the ideal child never includes a handicap of any kind. And realistically, a learning problem can be costly—in time as well as in dollars. Help with homework, extra lessons, visits to psychologists and physicians can be a heavy drain on the family budget. The disability imposes a burden on parents they did not expect and surely would not have planned. In many families, however, parents are not completely surprised when a child has trouble learning. They can relate their difficulties either to their own earlier problems or to those of other relatives. "He's just like me. I never could spell and I still can't write so anyone can read it," is a frequently-heard comment.

But what about the adopted child? Parents can't possibly trace the source of his difficulties. Perhaps that is why it is even harder for these parents to live with and understand a child's learning difference. Then, too, expectations may be even higher and the disappointments more keen for an adopted child than when the baby is born to parents. It must be hard to have waited a long time for a child who turns out to be less than perfect and who may not be able to fulfill all his parents' fantasies.

Lucille, a former student of mine, was adopted when her parents had been married for six years, after they had come to terms with their childlessness. Lucille entered the family at the age of two months and seemed to be all they had hoped for. Then, much to their amazement, they had a natural child when Luci was three years old.

Much love and attention had been lavished on Luci before the birth of her sister and, when the baby was born, Luci seemed to accept her with her usual good nature. She was her mother's eager helper and did not seem to resent the attention given the infant.

As a toddler, Luci was an active, supercharged little girl who needed a great deal of supervision to keep her out of mischief. She was one of those wiry children who are "into everything" and never seem to slow down. The birth of the baby seemed to enhance that restless quality. Luci's parents found themselves running after her more than ever. When she was five years old, the family asked me to test her because they were concerned about the problems that the kindergarten teacher had brought to their attention. Luci had apparently become dependent and whiny in class and her skills were not up to those of the other children.

When I saw Luci in my office, the first thing I noticed was how hard it was for her to sit still and pay attention. She jumped around, touching everything in sight, opening every drawer and cabinet. My testing showed that she was lagging behind in skills as well and did, indeed, have learning problems.

Her parents had been concerned only about her behavior but now we all agreed it would be important to work with her on learning skills as well. After seeing Luci for a while, I was pleased with her academic progress. However, I could see that her relationship with her parents had begun to deteriorate, almost from the day I explained the nature of her problems to them. They seemed increasingly impatient with her and favored her younger sister more and more. Luci began to lose some of her bubbly spontaneity and was becoming sullen and angry at home.

As she had done before, one day when she was eleven Lucille marched into my office and announced, "I'm going to run away to find my real mother. This family is just too mean to me." Usually her anger was directed toward her mother and they fought a great deal. During one of these bouts, Lucille's mother had become so angry she had even locked the girl out of the house. She had apparently become so upset and bewildered that she had responded childishly.

After that incident, I met with Luci's mother and father more regularly to talk about family issues. They needed an opportunity to discuss the feelings Luci stirred up in them. Somehow, the stigma of having an adopted child who also had learning disabilities was more than they had bargained for. They were sure that everyone was talking about what a "loser" Luci was as, perhaps, by association, they were too.

Luci also was burdened. She was a bright enough child to know how much she had slipped in her parents' estimation. Consequently, she often acted out her frustration, getting into fights with the neighbors as well as her own family. When she attempted to run away, she had the fantasy that she would find her loving birth mother and at last would be somebody's favorite child. This is not an uncommon fantasy among all children during periods of stress, but it is particularly potent for the adopted child.

I tried to help Luci's parents see how much they were hurting her by their lack of acceptance. Luci was striking out because she felt both criticized and excluded. It was understandable that Luci's family should feel disappointed in her lack of achievement, but their attitude was destructive. It wasn't easy, but her parents came to realize that it was up to them to try to restore Luci's former cheery good nature and positive self-image. She had to be invited back into the family circle, in spite of her learning disabilities. Luckily, her family understood and were able to give her what she needed.

Luci's family gave me the unusual opportunity of following her from early childhood to adulthood. Watching her develop into a delightful young woman was further verification of the importance of the family in the life of the child with learning disabilities. If I had ever thought the school could do it alone, this family certainly proved otherwise.

Life within any family can be complicated by a child's learning disability. What starts as a problem in the classroom may spill over and affect everything else. Whether a child is adopted, an only child or one of many, an angry little boy or a slow-moving little girl, there are few areas of life that remain untouched. And the problems of living together as a family may become even more intensified as children become adolescents and young adults.

Here are a few generally useful dos and don'ts for parents of LD youngsters of any age:

1. Rules and limits are important. Be sure your child understands what is expected of him and that you're not asking more of him than he can accomplish. On the other hand, don't let his learning disability be an excuse for non-performance. In areas where he feels relatively secure, perhaps he can strive to do more.

2. Open communication between parent and child always helps, though communicating doesn't necessarily come easily. In moments when you're not upset, try to open the channels. Share with your child some of your feelings and thoughts about his role in the family. Be sure to listen to his ideas too.

3. Help other members of the family understand the LD child's problems and his differences. Family secrets only serve to confuse everyone.

4. Don't feel guilty and blame yourself for your child's learning disability. It isn't your fault, and besides, guilt isn't a productive emotion. What your child needs is your support and love. (And what you might need is an occasional day away from all the problems at home. Be good to yourself.)

5. Don't insult the child who's misbehaving. Criticism and sarcasm are painful weapons, particularly when used in front

of others. Try to focus on the *behavior* that is unacceptable rather than the child himself. Appropriate behavior is learned, not necessarily built-in. Be clear and consistent about discipline. Threats and "or else"s only serve to confuse a child if they are not followed through. And for those few times when a parent feels he has misjudged his child, a sincere apology can go a long way toward strengthening parent-child relationships.

6. Be prepared to accept the disorganization and absent-mindedness that often accompany learning disabilities. LD children may need much repetition and frequent reminders of their responsibilities. Chances are, they really are not forgetting on purpose, although you may doubt this at times.

7. Set up situations to foster constructive social behavior at home. Organizing family projects can encourage a spirit of cooperation more than individually assigned chores. A "we" orientation can make even onerous jobs more pleasant.

8. Verbalize social values for children. Avoid lectures, but let your child know you notice when he has acted honorably, and conversely that you disapprove when he cheats on a test or lies to a friend.

9. Encourage your child to think about how other people feel and try to teach empathy and compassion by discussion as well as by example.

10. Discuss alternate ways of dealing with interpersonal conflicts. Asking the child, "What else could you have done?" may be more constructive than scolding.

11. Praise for effort can act as an impetus for working toward desired goals. A child will try harder if he feels his accomplishments, no matter how small, are noticed.

12. Keep a sense of humor. Family life, especially with an LD child, can be pretty hard without it. Making light of minor disasters and faux pas can help keep the family in balance.

The following list was distributed by a chapter of the Association for Children and Adults with Learning Disabilities (ACLD). It seems to me worth sharing:

1. Blessed are parents who listen to their children, for they in turn will be heard.

2. Blessed are they who do not expect more of their children than is appropriate for their level of maturity, for they shall not be disappointed.

3. Blessed are parents who do not attempt to tackle the new math, for they shall not fail.

4. Blessed are parents who can laugh at themselves, for their children will laugh with them and not at them.

5. Blessed are the parents who may be called "old-fashioned." They can be assured they are on the right track, for so have children persecuted parents for generations, and their opinions will change by the time they are old enough to pay taxes.

6. Blessed are they who teach their children to understand and love each other, for they shall not get caught in the crossfire of a sibling war.

7. Blessed are the parents who let their children do for themselves what they are capable of doing, for they shall not be merely unpaid servants.

8. Blessed are the parents who take their children with them often, for they shall see the world with fresh eyes.

9. Blessed are the father and mother who have found success-outlets for their energies, for they will not need their children as status symbols or as justifications.

10. Blessed are the parents who do not pretend to be perfect, for their children will not be disillusioned.

chapter
4

CRISIS
IN THE FAMILY

Almost every day has its crisis for the child with a learning difference. Both in school and outside, he learns to "take his lumps" without ever being sure from which direction they will come. Such everyday occurrences as a forgotten lunchbox, a difficult exam, or an insult from a brother can trigger anxiety and spoil yet another day. What then must happen to these children when they hit a *real* crisis in their lives, when everyone in the family is feeling inordinately pressured in the face of separation or divorce, illness or death, or a move to another community? Such events are disorienting for everyone, but for the child with learning problems they are usually worse, causing great disruption in his or her life. While no two children respond similarly to crises, the one with learning disabilities may be less able to understand, less adaptable, and less controlled in his behavior. And he may not even have the language skills to talk about his feelings.

Marital problems, from incompatibility to separation and divorce, seem to be almost epidemic in our society. They are difficult for everyone involved, especially for children, and most especially for children who have problems of their own. On the other hand, most psychiatrists agree that divorce per se does not necessarily cause emotional problems for children. In fact, the child living with unhappily married parents may get into more difficulty than one where a divorce has been handled well.

I have often wondered when I meet children with learning problems from broken—or breaking—homes, which came first, the disability or the marital discord. Did the strain and worry about his parents overburden the child so that his ability to learn was affected? Or did the child's problems bring extra stress to an already difficult relationship? It's hard to know, but in several families I have seen, a child's handicapping condition was apparently more than the marriage could withstand. Rather than strengthening the bonds between husband and wife, it tended to sever them.

Parents need strength, imagination, and many resources to cope with the child with special needs. Some people, realizing the added stress their child is placing on their relationship, have sought support from outside, in the form of pastoral guidance, marital counseling, or psychotherapy. I have seen this kind of help forestall what seemed to be an imminent family split.

But where parents do separate, we have to recognize the impact that it may have on a learning-disabled child and be aware of the telltale signs of stress. A child may not even know how much he is affected by the changes in his life, but his behavior may make it quite apparent.

Jeffrey appeared to have had language disabilities long before his parents separated when he was ten. He was the younger of two boys with an achieving older brother. Jeff had always felt incapable of living up to the family image of excellence. In my sessions with him, we had concentrated on heavy doses of language training and reading comprehension. He knew of his parents' impending divorce, but we didn't spend much time discussing it since he seemed to accept the idea.

One day, however, we were talking about the Civil War as our country's greatest conflict. Jeff seemed particularly restless and uncomfortable. Before I could finish a sentence of explanation, he would say, "I don't understand." This became a kind of litany, over and over—"I don't understand." Finally, feeling impatient, I turned to him and asked rather crossly, "But what is it you don't understand?"

"How can they fight like that when they're like all in the same family?" was his almost teary reply.

The parallel suddenly became quite clear. Jeff was having a very painful time understanding "war" on any level. He was hurt and had closed many cognitive doors for himself in order to avoid any more pain. It took long hours of talk for the two of us to understand how his parents' problems were affecting his thinking—and certainly his work at school. At first, Jeff had thought it was the other way around; his learning problems were responsible for the unhappiness at home and even his parents' divorce. Guilt is not an uncommon emotion for children, and it seems to come in particularly heavy doses for youngsters with learning disabilities. Perhaps because they feel guilty about not being able to live up to family standards, they are ready to assume the responsibility for almost any parental disappointment or frustration.

Jeff told me that his parents had always fought a lot about what was best for him. They disagreed about his coming to see me, whether he should be in a special class in school, and how he should spend his summers. He had overheard so many arguments that he was convinced the divorce, too, was his fault. He needed to understand that his parents' problems were their own and had little to do with him.

Even older children who comprehend the reasons for parents' separation may have practical problems that affect their relationships with parents. I remember that Richard, at fifteen, was not surprised when his parents finally separated. He told me he had been expecting it for years. He seemed well prepared to handle the idea that his parents were incompatible and would be better off apart, but what we hadn't counted on were the everyday problems that the divorce presented for Richard.

Richard's father had been granted flexible visitation rights. According to the terms of the divorce, he could see Richard whenever he wished. He tended to be rather casual about his comings and goings, often calling Richard at the last minute.

Although Richard loved to be with his father, he found the erratic scheduling both annoying and upsetting. Like many LD youngsters, Richard managed best when routines were established and he could know what to expect. He and I had worked hard over the years to develop a workable structure for him, and he had finally become relatively well-organized as a teenager. Suddenly he found himself having to be free whenever his dad was available. His well-planned homework schedule was going by the board, along with his feeling of security.

Children without learning problems might be more flexible under such circumstances, but for Richard this wasn't possible. He was disturbed and resentful. When we talked, Richard's father understood what was bothering his son. He agreed to set up more regular visits that Richard could count on each week, and he usually let the boy have a say in what they would do together. Thereafter, Richard regained his composure and certainly his warm feelings for his dad.

Not all family conflicts are as easy to resolve as Richard's was. Some parents who are living apart keep the children in the crossfire of their own anger far more than Richard's parents did. Youngsters with learning problems are particularly vulnerable to this, since their perception and judgment are often somewhat faulty. They may not be able to sort out who is doing what to whom and why the conflicts are still taking place. As a result, they live in a constant state of confusion, anxiety, and anger.

Parents who find themselves caught up in interpersonal problems before, during, or after a separation may need to give particular attention to how the additional pressure is affecting their LD child. Parents going through a divorce may sometimes lose self-control and behave erratically. For LD children who particularly need stability and consistency, this can have dire effects.

While it certainly can be painful to discuss family problems, it is usually far better for the child to have a realistic idea of what is happening than to be kept in the dark, imagining the worst. Children can accept an honest explanation far more easily than their own frightening fantasies. And the frank discussion can open the door to those questions parents might never have anticipated.

In his book *The Boys and Girls Book About Divorce,* Dr. Richard Gardner has set forth some helpful and practical guidelines for parents that apply to all children—LD or not. The key word is *honesty.* Dr. Gardner claims, too, that openness between parent and child, regardless of the circumstances, inevitably helps the psychological climate in the family.

Sometimes parents don't want to prejudice their children against their ex-mates, so they talk about them in unrealistic and even glowing terms. Painting the missing spouse as practically perfect just doesn't make sense. Obviously, it's not so. If it were, a child might logically ask, "If Dad is so great, how come you got a divorce?"

On the other hand, there is the tendency to confide all one's troubles to a child, particularly the oldest in the family. This naturally increases in proportion to the loneliness of the divorced or abandoned spouse. While it is best to be honest, a sharing of the facts may need to be balanced with discretion. Young children are not really equipped to understand or to live with all the trauma their parents may be facing.

In some families, the child himself will try to help a parent through a lonely and difficult time by attempting to take the place of the absent mother or father. It's all too easy for an unhappy parent to allow this to happen, perhaps even to enjoy it. But it's a trap to avoid. A young child has a lot of growing up to do and should not be considered a replacement part, even temporarily.

A common fantasy children have is that the absent parent will return and eventually their parents will reunite. Some in this situation have told me they were imagining how things would be when their parents got back together again. This fruitless daydream only puts off the acceptance of things as they are. Unless this acceptance comes, a child can never reconcile himself to new relationships in a parent's life. It is important to make it clear to the child that, although his parents aren't enemies, they are probably not going to live together again.

Perhaps it is hardest of all for a child when a parent doesn't visit and appears to be disinterested in him. Again, a realistic approach is important. There is no point in trying to make excuses for the lack of parental attention in the hopes of sparing the young child some hurt. It is better to explain carefully that it is not the child's fault that the parent went away. It simply means that the missing parent may not be able to care enough for anyone or give what the child craves. The parent at home might say to a child, "It's going to be really rough for a while, but Mom [or Dad] has some problems that keep her from being able to see you. I know it hurts, though."

This may be a time when parents want some professional guidance to help a youngster adjust to an apparent rejection. It takes careful handling to get past such a blow to a young ego, but actually, children are far less fragile than most people realize and more capable of accepting painful realities than is generally recognized. What is more difficult for them to cope with is parental furtiveness, not being told what is going on and why it is happening. Half-truths only produce confusion and distrust.

Twelve-year-old Louise presented the opposite kind of problem surrounding divorce: she had two sets of parents, two homes and a great deal of concern from both. Step-parents usually mean well, but when they take on someone else's LD child, they have a lot to learn in a hurry. Few people can anticipate what it is like to have a child with problems until they actually are in the situation.

Louise loved spending summers with her father and step-mother. She looked forward to June when she could travel to her second home some distance away. She had made a few summer friends through the years and usually had a good time at the local day camp near her dad's house—partly because few people there knew of her learning problems. It was during these annual visits, when I tutored her, that I had gotten to know Louise.

Last summer Louise began to balk at the reading her father assigned. One evening, her stepmother, Mrs. Valetti, called to tell me that the family was at swords' points over Louise's "homework". Not only was she refusing to read, but she had angrily lashed out at Mrs. Valetti when reminded to do her assignment, "You're not my mother. I don't have to take orders from you!" Louise and her stepmother had always had a good relationship and Mrs. Valetti had felt like a parent, at least in the summer.

Mrs. Valetti told me she didn't know how to respond to Louise's unforeseen attack. "She was always such an easy, good kid," she said. She also did not like the idea that her husband was caught in the middle of their conflict.

The Valettis' concern about Louise's reading was understandable. They felt responsible for Louise during the summer and didn't want her to lose ground academically. It is well known that youngsters with learning disabilities need more reinforcement and practice than other kids to retain the skills they've mastered during the school year. A poor memory is one of the common symptoms of LD, regardless of age.

I realized, however, that Louise's angry outburst at her stepmother was probably just the tip of the iceberg. She had been a good sport about her learning problems, had willingly been tutored summer and winter for years. Now she was fed up, reading assignments and all. Everyone was too conscious of her difficulties at a time when she needed to put the emphasis on the positive. At twelve she was old enough to want to seem "perfectly normal" to her parents as well as to her friends. And she wanted to spend her free time with kids, not with books.

Mrs. Valetti and I discussed the idea that perhaps she was trying too hard to be the "good mother," to do everything right. It is not easy to find a happy medium when you're a stepparent, especially a seasonal one. When stepparents see children only part-time, there tends to be a diminished intimacy. When children are little, treats and special events can fill the void, but as they get older there may be less communication and understanding. Some teenagers have said they began to feel like visitors in their "second" homes, an uncomfortable position for them as well as for their parents.

For most older children, one mother is quite sufficient. Mrs. Valetti wisely began to back off from the mothering role to become Louise's friend. Reading, after all, was not the essence of their relationship. Louise's father decided that instead of making an issue of the reading over the summer, he could find other ways to help Louise learn and grow. The family took an interesting trip for which they read maps and guidebooks. Louise's dad also made a pact with Louise that she could read on her own during the summer—with no questions asked—and could double up on her tutoring before school started in the fall.

It is not only the stepparents of LD children who need help with the dynamics of family situations. For example, when parents are merely quarreling and not even considering divorce, they cannot overlook the effect of their arguments on an LD child's already shaky sense of security. Parents in relatively stable families may need to reassure their youngsters, especially those with learning differences, that every argument does not necessarily lead to a family breakup. That is often the first thought that occurs to a child when his parents are fighting. Almost every youngster I have seen professionally has, at some time, expressed fear or lingering doubt about the permanence of his parents' marriage. Divorce has become an almost universal fantasy for children. It has to be recognized and dealt with. And when learning is difficult for a child, the whole world seems a little unstable and unreliable.

Children can suffer separation and loss in many ways. The most difficult is undoubtedly the death of a parent or caretaking adult. Since a child's basic fear is for himself, inevitably, the loss of anyone close is a reminder of the possibility that he too could die. He also has an understandable concern about who will take care of him if he is abandoned.

Actually, the permanence of death is an issue that few of us are able to face easily. Regardless of age or maturity, death is the topic most likely to be avoided. For example, many people who have learned to be open with children about the beginnings of life and the reproductive process have great difficulty discussing the end of the life cycle. No family is immune to the death of someone close, but almost all of us try to protect our children from these experiences. Too often we say, "He's too young to understand," or "Let's not worry him. Why should he suffer?" Maybe we are really trying to protect *ourselves* from grief and pain by avoiding any discussion or explanations.

The perception of death and loss is confusing for all children, but for the child with learning differences, who usually can only understand the here and now, a death in the family may be even more incomprehensible and terrifying. He may be unable to see the cause and result of an illness or an accident and only know that someone he loves has disappeared.

Most modern children have been bred on the violence they have seen on television. Saturday morning cartoons may seem innocent enough, but most of them are filled with tales of aggression and terror. As children get older, they watch real-life situations in which killing is commonplace. As a result, youngsters with learning disabilities may not be able to distinguish the death that comes as a natural culmination of living from the gory deaths they have seen in cartoons or murder mysteries. One article quotes a child who, looking at dead flowers his mother had discarded, asked what happened to them. When his mother replied that they had died, he wanted to know, "Who shot them?"*

It is probably easier for parents and children when a

*Crase, D. D., "Helping Children Understand Death." *Young Children,* Nov. 1976, Vol. 32, no. 1., p. 211.

child's first experience with death is the loss of a pet. Many valuable lessons can be learned if the death is not dismissed lightly and the child's grief is not diminished by an anxious parent. It is tempting for parents to replace the lost animal immediately in hopes that their child's suffering will end. In a way, though, this robs the child of the opportunity to deal with his grief over the loss. It helps when a child can bury his pet with some ceremony and share his pain with his family. Perhaps this is a rehearsal for future experiences, but it is a healthy one.

Sometimes, though, the death of a pet is confused with other, earlier losses in the family. This happened to Ellen, a sweet little seven-year-old who had a mild reading problem. She was so embarrassed to read aloud in second grade, though, that her mother had called me to see if I could help. Ellen made slow, steady progress and was beginning to feel more sure of herself in school.

Then she seemed to undergo a sudden, almost overnight change. Without any apparent reason, she became a frightened, anxious child who would not leave home even to play with her friend next door. She also began to have frequent tantrums and some problems falling asleep in her own room. When Mrs. Smith and I tried to figure out what might have happened to upset her, we could come up with nothing more serious than the death of her pet bird, Budgy, who had been buried in a shoe-box in the back yard.

Ellen had seemed to accept Budgy's death with equanimity. Yet, now, weeks later, she covered her ears and ran out of the room if Budgy's name was mentioned. No one had thought much about this until one day when Ellen told me she had had a terrible nightmare. She had dreamed that her grandmother, who had died the year before, was buried with Budgy in the shoe-box. As we talked, it seemed that many of Ellen's feelings about the loss of her grandmother were surfacing around the loss of her pet. She had loved her grandmother and had never talked about how she missed her.

When Ellen's mother and I talked of her grandmother's death, I realized that there had been no discussion with Ellen at the time, since the Smiths felt that a six-year-old "should not have to deal with so much sadness." Ellen was sent to stay at a cousin's house all through the mourning period. When she returned home, it was as though nothing had happened. Grandmother was seldom mentioned, in fact, and certainly not by Ellen. The death might have been more real to her had she participated in the traditional ceremonies and customs surrounding the funeral. These traditions help all of us put a close to a life that has ended.

Mrs. Smith had assumed incorrectly that Ellen was untouched by grief because nothing was mentioned. However, Ellen was not a very talkative child and she had always found it difficult to tell how she felt. With emotional stress, she became even more reticent. So for Ellen, her grandmother's death remained unfinished business.

It is not unusual for children to react differently from adults when there is a loss. It may take a long time for a child to realize the finality of what has happened and to feel the sadness that grown-ups comprehend immediately. That may be why some children are able to go on cheerfully as if nothing occurred when everyone around them is gloomy and depressed. Some children may also react to death or illness with anger, fear, or depression. Whether a child has a learning disability or not, it is hard to predict when one or the other mood will be upon him. Just as with adults, there is a process to be gone through before the crisis is finally resolved. Knowing that these are the normal components of grief can be helpful to a family trying to lead a child through a painful time.

Chronic illness in the family represents another kind of crisis a child may have to live through. Any illness is a threat to a child's security, particularly if it is the caregiving parent who can no longer fulfill that role. But as hard as it is for a child to accept a sick parent or grandparent, it is perhaps even more poignant when a sibling has an accident or debilitating illness.

An unusual situation occurred with one of my students whose brother was in and out of hospitals with a chronic kidney disease. There was always the realistic fear that he might not live very long. For Peter, the double burden of his learning disability and his worry about his brother created almost unbearable stress. Every time his brother was hospitalized, his teacher noted a significant drop in his schoolwork. What amazed his family, though, was that Peter rarely appeared worried or frightened, the emotions they expected under the circumstances. Instead he seemed angry much of the time. His rages were too much for his parents to handle during that particular period, and they found themselves responding in kind. While that was understandable, I tried to help them see that anger is not an uncommon reaction when children are frightened and confused. It is one of their outlets when they can't openly express their feelings.

When Peter and I talked about what was going on at home, he burst into tears and said he didn't know why he was so angry either. He really was "so scared," he said. Peter and I also recognized that he was furious with his brother for getting sick and terribly frightened that he might die. True, his brother had been a "pain in the neck" before the illness, but, Peter said, "I didn't hate him all that much! Why did he have to get so sick?" Unconsciously, Peter was assuming some of the blame for his brother's condition. He needed to know that he had absolutely nothing to do with it, even though he had sometimes wished his brother the worst.

We talked about how guilty Peter felt because he was healthy and at the same time, how angry he was at his brother for getting all the attention. Peter's feelings were confused, to be sure, but not entirely inappropriate or unusual in response to such a traumatic situation.

We could not change the reality of his brother's illness, but we did try to help Peter accept it. It is perhaps the most difficult situation a child has to deal with—the illness or death of someone in his own generation. A child's first view of his own mortality raises many questions and fears. And an adult's awareness and understanding of the significance of such an experience can help him handle it better.

There are obviously other crises that arise from time to time in any family. These might include moving, the birth of a sibling, a parent out of work, or an extension of the immediate family to include an older, perhaps infirm relative. Any of these events might cause a wrench in a household. More attention may need to be paid to helping the child with learning differences understand the changes that are taking place and how they will affect him. He should be brought into the picture so he clearly knows how he is involved. Sometimes we take for granted that a child knows what is occurring, but in my office, I am frequently surprised at the confusion and lack of comprehension that exist for so many of these youngsters. If they have difficulty with abstract reasoning or cause-and-effect relationships, they may have no idea why the family is moving or when the event will take place. "Three months from now" has very little meaning for a child who cannot tell time or who may have an inadequately developed concept of the duration of time.

The parents of one young child gleefully announced one day, "We are moving from New York to Los Angeles because Dad is being transferred." As it turned out, the boy assumed that the "we" meant only his mother and father. He apparently worried so much that he developed a skin rash along with insomnia, but he could not explain why he was upset. When his parents finally understood what the problem was, they tried to assure him that he would be going with them. They showed him pictures of the new house, but it was only the promise of a much-wanted dog that satisfied him and allayed his fears. This story is just one more example of how concrete an LD child's thinking can be.

When I last saw this lad, he was scared to go to the new school where teachers would not know about his learning disability and his problems with reading. I assured him that I had spoken to his new teacher as well as the resource teacher in his new school and that reassured him a little.

Living in a family, then, through good times and bad, may require a lot of thought and many adjustments on everyone's part. Of course, it is up to parents to set the tone but sometimes, in the midst of a problem, it is too easy to forget the positives in life. To a child, and to an LD child particularly, a crisis may make it seem that all good things have come to an end forever. No one will ever be happy again. During times like that, the mutual support that comes from sharing happy memories and making plans for the future may be what is needed for the family to get past the bad times.

chapter
5

THE SOCIAL SIDE
OF SCHOOL

"We have thirty-one kids in our class, but I feel like I'm all alone. I guess it's because I'm the only one with a learning disability." This is what Chris told me one day. In all probability, he was *not* the only one in his class with learning problems, but he apparently couldn't notice anyone else's when his own were so overwhelming. Chris had been "mainstreamed," that is, placed in a regular fifth-grade class, a few months earlier and he was, indeed, having a hard time—socially as well as academically. He was proving all over again what I had long suspected, that even in a crowded classroom, school can be the loneliest place of all for a child with a handicap.

While school represents a positive socializing experience for many youngsters, it can also be socially destructive. If a child has learning problems to begin with and always seems to be the odd man out, his life in school can easily become a nightmare—as Chris's was. Not only was he the youngster with "special needs" in the classroom, he also had to leave to go to the "resource room" for part of each day. A resource room is a center within the school to which children are referred for specific help in areas of need. Youngsters identified as having learning disabilities can spend as much time there in the course of a day as is warranted, working one-to-one or in a small group with an LD specialist. Going to the resource room was certainly necessary for Chris, but it

made him look even more "special" to the other children—
and he and they resented it.

With the current trend toward integrating LD children
into regular classrooms, children may suffer more from social differences than from scholastic problems. As one ten-
year-old put it, "The only way I can live is because I think
of vacations and getting away from the kids who hate me in
school."

Children with all sorts of handicaps are often rejected by
their classmates and even, unwittingly at times, by their
teachers. Study after study has shown that children with
learning disabilities generally are considered to have the lowest social status in a class. This may have started with their
earliest school failures or even before—perhaps when they
were toddlers in the sandbox. They may never have learned
how to get along with children their own age, because of their
own immaturity and their troubles in communicating.

Being out of step presents problems for children at home
and in the neighborhood, but it can be most devastating in
the classroom where social pressures are intense and ongoing
through the day. From first graders to high school seniors,
I hear the recurring plaint from young people with learning
problems, "The kids just don't like me."

When I ask, "What makes you think so?" inevitably they
come forth with some poignant evidence. Kevin, who is six,
says the children steal his lunch, leaving him nothing to eat.
He is afraid to tell his teacher so he goes hungry. Twelve-
year-old Helen is teased and called nasty nicknames because
of her pimples and braces. And Lynn, at sixteen, is tormented in the gym locker room where a group of girls threat-
ens to beat her up.

These three youngsters have almost nothing in common—
except their learning disabilities and the social problems that
plague them. Kevin refuses to go to school, Helen's best
friend is the school nurse, and Lynn says she is so scared,
she's afraid to walk through the corridors to classes.

Although a regular class in a local school is considered to

be the "least restrictive environment" according to federal guidelines, it may not be so for some LD youngsters, particularly if they turn out to be the least accepted members of the class. Merely placing children physically in the mainstream will not necessarily integrate them into the class or cure their social deficits. In fact, studies have shown that non-handicapped children interact very little with their handicapped peers and frequently regard them as the "untouchables" in the class. Moreover, LD children don't seem to acquire social skills vicariously from the classmates who ignore them. They usually need much more than exposure to learn appropriate behavior. They need instruction and a great deal of practice to improve their social skills.

Sometimes the mainstream may actually increase a child's social isolation and represent a *more* restrictive environment for a child than a special class which can provide the support and social acceptance the LD youngster needs. When everyone else is more or less in the same boat, it is easier to feel a sense of belonging. And being more readily accepted in a group can give a child the chance to practice social skills and learn how to get along with others. He may even begin to learn how it feels to be popular.

Children who are popular with their peers have some characteristics in common. They seem to know intuitively how to make friends. They probably appeal to others because they are more self-confident, outgoing, and cooperative than less accepted youngsters. They are also likely to be empathetic, supportive, and generous with their friends. Many LD children do not have these qualities. They may be too self-involved to help a friend, or lack the confidence and know-how to reach out to others in appropriate ways. And most of all, their repeated failures in school make other youngsters look down on them—particularly if they are in regular classrooms.

With the lack of understanding and the stigma attached to a learning disability (or any handicap), these children often live in a social world that is qualitatively different from that of their peers. They may be teased about their problem, left out when everybody's choosing up sides, made a scapegoat, or totally ignored.

The discontent and frustration associated with mainstreaming may not be confined to students. Teachers, too, may feel keenly the burden it imposes on them. They can be required to integrate "exceptional" children in their classes without adequate preparation or planning. A teacher accustomed to a well-formulated program may suddenly find herself at the head of a cliquey, chaotic classroom. She may feel angry and even depressed. I have spoken to teachers who are more than willing to individualize instruction and adapt to new methods of teaching, but who find it impossible to adjust to a variety of behaviors they've never had to cope with before. Their newest students may seem to need a good course in human relations far more than a modified curriculum!

Chris was in a regular first-grade class when his learning problems were identified. If he had only had problems with reading, he probably could have stayed in the regular class, but he was also aggressive and disruptive. He bothered the other children, cried if he didn't get his way, and occasionally even kicked his teacher in frustration.

In January of that year, it was decided that a small, special class was the only answer for Chris. He was moved two weeks later to an LD class in a school a short bus ride away. (Incidentally, I have noticed that when younger children are recommended for special education, more often than not, it is because of their behavior and social maladjustment even more than their academic problems.)

In the three-and-a-half years that Chris spent in the LD class, he made good progress. His skills were better and he had calmed down to the extent that his teacher thought he could manage in a regular class.

At first, after he was switched, Chris seemed rather shy but not unhappy. He tried hard to complete assignments and keep up with his homework. Ms. Russell, the fifth-grade teacher, had welcomed the challenge of having Chris in her class. She had volunteered to take him and was pleased with his progress. As the weeks went on, though, she became aware that Chris was out of his seat more than he was in it and that he was not making friends. In fact, he was beginning to collect enemies. School aides also reported that Chris was causing trouble during recess and that he usually ate lunch alone. He couldn't seem to handle change and became disruptive. When there was a substitute teacher in the class, Chris was invariably the one sent to the principal's office.

In class, Chris was reverting to some of his old habits. He hummed during spelling tests and annoyed those who sat near him until everyone asked to move away. During quiet reading time, there would be only one sound in the classroom —Chris rhythmically tapping his fingers or feet. When asked to stop, he either couldn't or wouldn't, and he actually seemed surprised that he was annoying anyone. He was getting less and less work done during the school day, and kept insisting that it was because the other kids were "bothering" him.

Ms. Russell realized her feelings had gotten out of hand one afternoon when she grabbed Chris's arm and dragged him out of the room. She felt helpless, angry, and very disappointed. She had had high hopes for her first mainstreaming experience, and now was ashamed that she couldn't hide her anger at Chris.

At the next faculty meeting, she somewhat reluctantly discussed her predicament with the staff. She was embarrassed to admit her defeat with Chris, but at the same time was eager for suggestions. Ms. Russell was relieved to find that she was not alone—other teachers had been in the same situation, and were just as disturbed about it. It is one thing to recognize the special academic needs of LD students, but quite another to deal with their aberrant and sometimes antisocial behavior.

For the first time, Ms. Russell's principal recognized how unprepared the staff was to deal with the Chrises in the school. I think perhaps he had secretly hoped that main-streaming would somehow fall by the wayside before he and his teachers would have to become too involved with it. Since this wasn't happening, he asked me to come to school to meet with those teachers who wanted help. I welcomed the chance to do so, particularly since I was working privately with Chris and knew just how frustrated he was too.

The first thing I did was to observe Chris in the classroom. Previously, I had only seen him on a one-to-one basis in my office and I wanted to see where he stood in the social scheme of things. It was obvious within the first ten minutes that the lowest rung on the social ladder had been reserved for Chris —and he knew it. He tried to join a group of three boys chatting as they came into class, but they ignored him. Then, while taking off his jacket, Chris inadvertently hit a boy's shoulder—lightly. The boy retaliated with a swift punch which seemed to indicate just how he felt about Chris. Ms. Russell finally separated the boys with an accusing glance at Chris and told him to sit down.

From my spot in the back of the classroom I noted a few other things, too. When the class began to work, Chris didn't have his books and papers ready and he had apparently misplaced his pencil. Then he couldn't seem to find the right page in his spelling book and was soon way behind the others. He seemed so perturbed by this time that he apparently didn't hear Ms. Russell's instructions. He leaned over to ask each of his neighbors what to do, which annoyed the boys and girls around him. They were probably also afraid to talk since Ms. Russell had insisted on quiet during work-time. So even if they had wanted to help Chris—which they didn't—it would have been against the rules.

When the other kids tried to ignore Chris, he pushed even harder. He repeated his question, louder and more frantically this time, and finally grabbed one boy's paper off his desk. By that time, Chris seemed so anxious to get the answers, he didn't care how he got them. Now he was in trouble with Ms. Russell as well as his neighbors. And so went the morning.

When the bell rang for recess, Chris ambled to the door, almost the last to leave the room. The boy who had hit him earlier tripped him in the hall and a couple of girls giggled as Chris stumbled. "Flunked again, huh?" one of them jeered as she ran past.

In the half hour that followed recess, I watched Chris break his pencil point, get up to sharpen it, knock a book off his desk, rip a paper in frustration (which necessitated getting another), go to the bathroom, stare out the window, and, in general, accomplish nothing. It became clear that his teacher had not exaggerated when she had said that in the last few weeks, Chris was doing "no work in school."

A little later, Ms. Russell returned a set of science tests and announced to the class, "You really did well on this test— only one person failed." I watched thirty pairs of eyes turn toward Chris, though his name was never mentioned. Ms. Russell, knowing she had unwittingly humiliated Chris, tried to change the subject very quickly, but it was too late. He was slumped down in his seat with his eyes covered, a picture of abject sadness.

I left the classroom thinking of the many Chrises I knew with similar problems in school. What made Chris's own situation different, though, was that his teacher cared enough to try to change things. Help for youngsters with social problems has long been needed in education, but only recently have we begun to think of ways to effect this. There are actually many techniques to help a child feel more like a member of a class and minimize his social differences. The choice of strategy will depend on the child and his teacher's preference.

At the next meeting with the teachers, I told of my visit to Chris's classroom and what I had seen. One thing seemed apparent: if Chris were more organized about his work, he might be less of a nuisance to the other children. Ms. Russell agreed and suggested she could write out the daily schedule for Chris and check before class to see that he had the materials he needed. She also recognized that she had been coming down awfully hard on the boy recently. She might have to look long and hard, but she was sure she could find a few reasons to compliment him. I agreed, feeling that it was likely the youngsters in the class were emulating Ms. Russell's negative attitude toward Chris without realizing it. Her feelings were contagious. If she could change her own response, maybe the class would follow suit.

At first, Chris was suspicious. He ducked out of his early morning meetings with Ms. Russell whenever he could but she persevered in trying to gain his confidence. She understood he was so unhappy in class that he couldn't believe things would ever change. He couldn't even bring himself to ask Ms. Russell for help when he was stuck. This is so typical —and so frustrating for teachers! Some children who need help the most are so embarrassed that they deny it—even to themselves. And they only sink deeper into the morass.

After a while, though, Chris began to be more responsive to his teacher because she was friendlier to him in class and had even asked him to run the movie projector. This was something he loved to do, but it had always been an honor reserved for the A students. Eventually, Chris and Ms. Russell could talk about how he had hated those first few isolated months at school.

When Ms. Russell called me to report on her progress with Chris, she felt that her own more positive attitude toward him was being picked up by the other children. They seemed a little more tolerant and not quite so critical. In fact, one of the boys seemed to have appointed himself "first assistant teacher," and was often on hand when Chris needed some answers, particularly after Ms. Russell said it was all right.

Teachers can play a crucial role in influencing a child's social status. In fact, their feelings toward a child with special needs often determine how that youngster is viewed by his peers. A teacher can embarrass a child or compliment him, support or denigrate him, enhance his self-image or destroy it. Many teachers may be surprised by the impact they have on children, but it is obvious that they do far more than teach academic subjects. They also teach attitudes.

In all honesty, I sometimes wonder about the way teachers treat children. I was visiting a gym class recently to observe a youngster. The boys and girls were waiting for the teacher to arrive and were giggling and talking in small groups when she entered. Suddenly, a loud ear-piercing whistle blew and she screamed at them, "Get in line immediately or I'll throw you all out of here!"

I'm certain that teacher would never have talked to an adult that way. When she saw me, she smiled and could not have been sweeter. I wondered how we can expect children to treat each other with respect when grown-ups treat them without any. Unfortunately, the youngsters in the class I saw did not even look surprised. Apparently they were used to that kind of treatment. And the boy I had come to visit went right on swearing at his neighbor. Why not, in such an atmosphere?

The teacher, as authority figure in a classroom, obviously does much to set the tone, but it also is true that children are influenced by their peers. Sometimes the peer culture can be even more powerful than adults in remedying a child's social disabilities.

Peer interaction, in fact, might be called the least utilized resource in education. Usually it is only the early childhood teachers in nursery schools and day-care centers who stress social values and learning from peers. Little children are taught to solve interpersonal conflicts and to be aware of the feelings of others. Once they enter the more "grown-up" school, however, this kind of learning ends. The system seems to dictate that teachers alone can impart values and skills in the classroom, and interaction between the children is discouraged. The interplay of children is usually felt to be appropriate only in gym and extracurricular activities. It is time, though, that we begin to appreciate the role children can play in teaching each other, all through the day, in the classroom as well as on the playground. Healthy peer relationships, after all, contribute to a youngster's future values and attitudes as well as to his mental health and intellectual ability as an adult.

One day, Ms. Russell and I were commenting on how well Chris had done since he had a buddy to work with in class. This one positive relationship was like the proverbial pebble in the stream. Acceptance for Chris had slowly begun to ripple outward. Before too long, he was not so obviously the odd man out and even his grades started to improve.

Ms. Russell said she was thinking of implementing a "buddy system" throughout her classroom, particularly for spelling and social studies projects. Because of her experience with Chris, she began to feel that perhaps she was unwittingly undermining healthy relationships in her class by stressing individual grades and competition. Cooperative learning, rather than competition, promotes academic achievement as well as social growth. For an LD youngster especially, individual competitive learning can be damaging to self-esteem. This is the child who almost never comes out first, and the combination of last one finished, lowest grades, and "see me" written on every paper is guaranteed to deflate an already fragile ego.

When children are paired to work together, no individual is being judged on his own. He is part of a team. Chris's buddy, an easygoing, popular boy, obviously enjoyed the responsibility for helping Chris. In turn, Chris glowed with the attention and began to take on some of the best qualities that he saw in his new friend. Children provide behavior models for one another. This can work out well or badly but Chris was lucky—he had a good model to emulate.

Several weeks into the buddy system, Ms. Russell was aware that Peter, her most withdrawn and quiet child, seemed to be coming out of his shell a bit. She had been dubious about whether he would be able to work with someone else, but even he seemed to have benefited from the contact and communication with another student.

Peter was the kind of boy who could easily be overlooked. He had no friends in school and, in fact, one morning when

Ms. Russell had asked if Peter was absent, Janie had piped up, "Peter who?" That said it all.

Actually, Peter was often absent. "School phobia" had been a recurring problem for him over the years. There always seemed to be a low point in the winter when Peter would get so discouraged he just couldn't drag himself to school. He claimed sore throats, headaches and stomachaches until his mother was afraid he might really be ill. However, she couldn't get him off to school even when she didn't believe him. I have known several LD children over the years who have resorted to truancy. School phobia, of course, usually has deeper psychological implications, but for the child with learning disabilities, it may reflect his fear and loneliness at school.

Whenever he *was* in class, Peter slouched in his chair and did not volunteer for anything. His classmates had apparently gotten the message and were leaving him strictly alone, allowing him the privacy he seemed to prefer. Peter was certainly not disruptive, but he was cause for concern—and he was annoying! It was not what he did, but what he did *not* do that had bothered his teachers for years. Ms. Russell had tried hard to get Peter involved in classroom activities that year, but the more she tried to push, the more he withdrew, and the more the other children ignored him. Creating a situation through the buddy system, where Peter had to interact with a classmate rather than his teacher, seemed to motivate him to come to school and make it easier when he was there.

Both Chris and Peter were lucky to have been with Ms. Russell, a sensitive teacher who was willing to learn and try new techniques. Once she began to experiment, it was relatively easy to think of more ways to integrate Chris and Peter into the classroom. But what about the places in school where she had less control, such as the lunchroom, music class, and gym? These are often areas with their own social problems for LD children.

I'm thinking in particular of Jimmy, who could be counted on to upset Mr. Penna, the gym teacher, every gym period.

Jimmy was well known as a troublemaker in the school. In fact, he had once said, "I feel like I've been on probation since I was born." He would fling peanut butter on the ceiling in the cafeteria, throw rocks through windows, and he was always in a fight at recess. He usually did these deeds in the company of another boy who may even have set him up.

Perhaps because Jimmy was small for his age, it seemed to Mr. Penna that the boy was acting up in order to feel big and "macho." And he certainly got recognition. Jimmy had confided to Mr. Penna, "I've got to be best at something and the only thing I'm good at is trouble. In fact, I'm the king of trouble."

It was obvious to Jimmy that he could never be known for his academic success or physical prowess, so he figured out the one way he could gain notoriety. He didn't like the punishments that ensued, to be sure, but at least he was noticed. It is not uncommon for children with learning problems to turn to clowning and disruptive behavior in school. This is their way of diverting attention from their academic inadequacy. Like Jimmy, they seem to think that if they become the "hero" of trouble, people won't notice that they can't read or spell.

Mr. Penna told me he was desperate about Jimmy. He couldn't figure out whether the boy was being difficult on purpose, was unable to control himself, or was simply unaware of his effect on others. Whichever it was, the children were becoming increasingly angry and resentful of the inordinate amount of time that Mr. Penna had to devote to keeping Jimmy in line. They were constantly losing play time because of him. The kids also complained about the way Jimmy acted on the school bus, in the lunchroom, and at recess.

Class trips were a special disaster—when Jimmy was allowed to go. Most often, he was left behind because of some recent infraction at school. Actually, his teachers were relieved when they didn't have to take him along on trips. If they went to the zoo, he needed a "keeper" of his own, and at a museum, everyone was nervous as he sprinted carelessly past the exhibits. Jimmy always seemed particularly "hyper" when he was away from school and familiar territory.

Actually, trips were no fun for Jimmy either. He was usually banished to the back of the bus so he wouldn't bother the driver and, besides, no one wanted to sit with him anyway. It was always "twosomes" on trips except for Jimmy who remained a party of one. He generally ended up with the teacher or class mother as his partner, and that was not his idea of fun. Jimmy was the first to say that he hated class trips and would much rather stay at school. Those were the days he didn't have to work, but could run errands and help out in the kindergarten.

Mr. Penna, some of the teachers, and I tried to think of ways to change Jimmy's behavior as well as his reputation throughout the school. People always expected him to be in the center of trouble, even when he wasn't anywhere near it. We finally decided that Mr. Penna and Jimmy's classroom teacher would have a class meeting to see what could be done.

During gym period the next day, Mr. Penna asked the children to sit down on mats. He said there was something he wanted to talk to them about. With Jimmy's permission, he briefly explained the problem. He wondered how many children would be willing to help Jimmy stay out of trouble. He went around the circle and each child voted "yes" or "pass." There were only three "passes" and Mr. Penna noted that those who demurred were the ones who inevitably joined Jimmy in his escapades. Mr. Penna complimented the three on their honesty and agreed that it would be pretty hard to help someone if you were in trouble yourself.

After that, some specific suggestions were offered by the children. The four that seemed worth implementing were:

1. having Jimmy sit at lunch with a responsible child on each side to protect him;

2. calling a teacher right away if trouble seemed to be brewing in the lunchroom or on the playground;

3. making sure that Jimmy was included in a game during recess;

4. giving Jimmy the responsibility for the gym equipment. This meant he had to be on time, but it was a status job and worth it.

For the first few days under the new regime, all was quiet, including Jimmy. Then the inevitable happened. Jimmy was goaded into trying to add to the peanut-butter collection on the lunchroom ceiling. According to plan, his lunch neighbor made a beeline for the teacher on duty who appeared in the nick of time. Another day when a sixth grader provoked Jimmy into an argument at recess, a trio of companions rose to Jimmy's defense—but only with words. The fist fight was averted and Jimmy, a pleased look on his face, left the playground accompanied by his bodyguards.

Group meetings were continued as needed when problems arose, and very gradually Jimmy's behavior changed. He had two and then three "good days in a row," as he said. He even began to feel more accepted by the kids who were getting to know him for himself and not for his reputation. Jimmy was a nature buff who knew a great deal about rocks, plants, and bugs. He had discounted this as a talent, though, sure no one else would appreciate it. When we suggested he talk about his hobby to the other children, he said, "I know they'll think it's weird." When he did mention it, though, he was surprised that one or two boys wanted to go down to the pond with him after school to find specimens. (Jimmy's parents were also delighted since this interest kept him outside and away from the TV set after school.)

For youngsters with learning disabilities, the relationship between home and school is extremely delicate. Teachers need space to work without excessive interference from overly anxious parents, and parents have to make sure their children are in the hands of caring and competent teachers. There is no doubt that children's academic and social growth will be smoother if teachers and families can work toward a common goal, putting aside as much as possible any personality conflicts or defensiveness. Mistrust or a lack of contact leaves large gaps which children often fill with misinformation and misperceptions.

Communication between home and school does not necessarily involve a formal conference, but can take place spontaneously as needed. A telephone call or note can be the means through which a parent can advise a teacher of a problem, a need, or even good news. Teachers can report to parents in similar fashion, calling on them for help and sharing the kudos as well. Compliments sent home have a healthy way of multiplying. The child also should be informed of the alliance between his parents and his teachers—and feel that his opinions count too. If he knows the when and why of conferences, he will feel more included and perhaps less worried about what might be going on behind his back.

It is never too early in the school year for parents of LD children to request a meeting. Teachers often have as much trepidation as parents have at the start of a new year and an alliance established early can be reassuring to both. At the first conference, parents may have to do most of the talking. (They have known the child longer!) The teacher will usually want to hear about a child's home environment and how he functions in it—particularly when that child has problems. In all probability, social problems at school are not so different from those at home. If they are, it's worth finding out why.

As the year goes on, the balance changes and at a meeting teachers may contribute a lot more information about how the youngster is doing in school, socially as well as academically. The major challenge to the teacher is not *what* to say, but *how* to say it. It's essential to use clear language parents can understand. Professional jargon should be assiduously avoided.

It is also important to be honest with parents. Some teachers try to couch their concern or criticism in language that is too subtle to be understood. They are probably afraid of alarming parents or arousing their antagonism. Consequently, parents sometimes leave a conference almost as much in the dark as when they came. Parents, too, are sometimes wary of teachers' reactions to what they say. They worry that if they antagonize the teacher, he may take it out on the child.

Conferences between parents and teachers are often fraught with expectations and disappointment. Impressions are measured against hearsay in this tenuous joint-custody arrangement that usually lasts only one year. Teachers complain that parents "don't trust the school," and "those parents who need it most don't show up for conferences." There is some truth in this. Some parents cannot spare the time from work—or really don't want to hear the bad news. If possible, house calls may be in order—and well worth the extra effort. But parents who do come in want more than platitudes from teachers. They want to know about their child's problems with peers, participation in class activities, and, above all, whether the teacher likes their child and can be supportive. If the lonely youngster in school has at least one friend and ally, the teacher, that's a good beginning.

Thinking about a conference in advance can help to set goals and provide a framework for sharing. One teacher I knew sent home a questionnaire for parents to complete before coming to a meeting. While this may be too formal an approach in some circumstances, a tentative agenda can be helpful. The following are a few questions parents might want to ask a child's teacher if they aren't brought up. While they need not be rigidly adhered to, they might remind you of important areas to cover:

1. Does my child participate in group activities and class discussions, or is he a loner in the class?

2. Does he work independently or is he at the teacher's desk for help or reassurance too often?

3. How about work habits? Can he complete assignments on time or is he easily distracted and unable to concentrate?

4. Is he included in play at recess or is he turning his classmates off?

5. Does he willingly stay in class or does he slip away and hide out in the lavatory?

Once these social issues are explored, it should be "cinchy," as the kids say, to talk about scholastic progress.

Here are a few questions teachers may want to ask parents —and should. While they may seem somewhat intrusive, they do have implications for the classroom and are, therefore, important for teachers to pursue:

1. How does your child feel when he comes home from school? Tired? Cranky? Happy?

2. If he is unhappy, what does he complain about?

3. Does he do homework willingly or avoid it until the last minute? And can he do it alone or are his parents going through third grade again?

4. What does he do after school? How does he spend his time?

5. What is he like to live with at home? How would you characterize his personality? Moody? Explosive? Easygoing? Delightful?

6. How does he get along with children in the neighborhood? Is he a leader, a follower, or all alone?

A teacher armed with the answers to these questions will be in a better position to work with a child. Only recently, a sensitive fifth grader whose parents were going through a messy separation said through her tears, "This is the worst year of my life. But I'm glad I have Miss Zee for my teacher. She understands and I can always talk to her when I'm upset —and that's almost every day."

chapter
6

A SPECIAL POPULATION: GIFTED AND LD

"How can he be so smart and act so dumb?" is a question teachers ask when they find out that one of the most puzzling youngsters in their class has an IQ in the "very superior" or "gifted" range. There is a whole group of children with tremendous intellectual ability who simply are not succeeding in school. These youngsters may have learning disabilities. As with any other LD population, their problems come in different sizes and shapes. They may have reading, writing, or math disabilities, but frequently their social problems are their greatest handicap. Their superior intelligence, in fact, can even exacerbate their social difficulties. A youngster who is gifted may be looked upon as different from his peers, and if he also has a learning disability, he may not fit in anywhere—academically or socially. The brighter the child, the greater must be his frustration when he has trouble in school.

According to the Gifted and Talented Children's Education Act of 1978, the five classifications of giftedness are: intellectual, creative, artistic, leadership (social), and specific academic aptitude (e.g., math or science). A sixth, athletic aptitude, has been added more recently. Einstein, General Patton, Rodin, and Hans Christian Andersen—all of whom had learning disabilities—could be cited as examples of giftedness in some of these areas. A creatively gifted child may be dyslexic, while a highly verbal youngster can be perceptually impaired. The only difference in being gifted, perhaps, is that the gaps between ability and disability seem even wider than in other children.

Several years ago, I saw a gifted LD child whose problems had been apparent when he was a preschooler. He spoke beautifully and reasoned well, but he could not begin to do the simplest puzzles or recognize numbers. He also showed evidence of behavior and attention problems from the time he started kindergarten. He could not keep up with the kindergarten curriculum and the other children thought he was strange. His teacher described him as very bright—but "hyperactive, restless, immature, and disruptive." Yet he was reading at a fourth-grade level. She didn't know what to do with him so she referred him to the school psychologist for testing.

George was found to have an IQ of 153 on the Stanford-Binet—and a learning disability. The neurologist who was consulted confirmed the diagnosis of a perceptual handicap but recommended that George stay in a regular school program in view of his intelligence. Somehow George and his teacher survived the year, but it was touch-and-go all the way. And first grade was more of the same.

Halfway through second grade, George was beginning to compensate for his perceptual problems but his greatest deficits were in the area of social maturity. He got "Satisfactory" in most academic subjects on his report card, but straight "Needs Improvement" under personal development categories. He flunked "self-control," "uses time wisely," and "gets along with others."

Near the end of the year, his teacher strongly recommended a more structured class to George's parents, by which she meant, "Please take him out of here!" The special class for emotionally handicapped children in the district was an alternative, but that was not appropriate either, since many children in the class were known to be performing well below grade level. Since there were no classes for the LD gifted, it looked as if either George's intellectual needs or his social adjustment had to be sacrificed.

George's parents, the teacher, and I met to see what could be done so that George could stay where he was. We all agreed that a full day in the classroom was more than he could handle. Somehow, the day had to be broken up for him. Since he excelled in reading, it was decided to excuse him from the regular program (which bored him anyway) and send him to learn about the school's new computer. Within a few weeks, he and a few other small "whiz kids" began to hang around the computer room with an enthusiastic volunteer. George also spent some time in the resource room when either he or his teacher needed a respite.

I worked with George that summer, too, to try to bring his work habits and his intellect into closer alignment. Without the distractions of the classroom, he began to concentrate for longer periods of time and even do a little arithmetic on his own.

Fortunately, the third grade in George's school was set up so he had a chance to be with a team of teachers rather than just one. If the team is strong, this can be enriching for the gifted child—and less wearing for the teachers. The program continued to be modified for George and that year was the best he had had. Eventually, the normal process of maturation—and good educational planning—helped him settle down.

It is not uncommon, though, for gifted youngsters to fall by the wayside in classes that either are inappropriate socially or do not stimulate them intellectually. These are the children who are most likely to develop emotional and behavioral problems as they go on in school.

Perhaps Doug, whom I met when he was in sixth grade, was one of these casualties. He was doing little or no work in school, he had no friends, and he was even beginning to be in trouble with the law. His teacher said, "He's smart, but in the wrong way." Everyone at school was frustrated by Doug and I was worried about him.

Doug had a long history of school-related problems. Because he was considered "young" for his age and couldn't hold a pencil or crayon, he had been kept back for an additional year in kindergarten. As it turned out, this probably was the wrong prescription, since he was not challenged intellectually and little was done to help him mature socially. And at the end of the year that he repeated, he still could not cut, color, or write his name.

Six years later, when I saw Doug, he had learned to write his name, but not so anyone could read it. And even his best writing was peppered with spelling and punctuation mistakes. He had gotten through the first five years of school by listening, but now he had just about given up on that too. Social studies assignments and book reports were torturous affairs that he flatly refused to do.

The school was convinced Doug must be emotionally disturbed. Disturbed he was, but at the root of his problems was the vast discrepancy between what he knew and what he could communicate. He had a terrible self-image and wouldn't put himself to the test. The thought of failure was intolerable to him.

As soon as Doug entered my office, I noticed his clumsy gait. He couldn't seem to put one foot in front of the other without tripping over it and he couldn't skip or hop—most unusual for a boy his age. As we talked, he said that he hated school and when I asked him what he disliked most, he quickly replied, "The fact that I have to go." Bitter humor was one of his defenses and a sign of his intelligence as well. Doug admitted that he had not handed in a written assignment in months and he had run fresh out of alibis. He couldn't stand to write, he said, and he wasn't "learning anything anyhow. So what's to write about?"

Doug's teacher was furious with him for not handing in work and she let him know it daily. She told me on the phone that she was positive he could write better if he tried. There was no excuse, she said, for such a bright boy to be so lazy. He was "getting away with murder." Unfortunately, the school had not acknowledged Doug's learning disability because his reading scores were so high, and was only aware of his "laziness" and his social problems.

When I spoke to Doug's parents, they said they felt caught in the middle between the school and Doug. They felt sorry for their son, but tended to get angry with him too because of the constant complaints from school. At least he should *try* to do the work, they conceded. Actually, they had thought he had a learning disability for years before they consulted me. He had been sensitive to loud noises even as an infant, disoriented and clumsy on stairs, and he didn't learn to ride a bicycle, tie shoelaces, or tell time until he was almost eight years old. This did not fit with the fact that he could read at three and talk his way out of almost anything. He kept his parents on their toes intellectually but at the same time seemed so far behind other kids his age.

Through the years, Doug's parents had disagreed when the school insisted that his problems were strictly emotional. They figured that school must be at least part of the problem since he was so much easier to live with on weekends and in the summer. Most of their family fights revolved around Doug's schoolwork, either inadequately done or not done at all. Eventually Doug's parents gave in, though, and did seek psychological help as the school had suggested.

Doug was enjoying his sessions with the counselor and seemed to be benefiting from them. He was getting along somewhat better with the kids at school and wasn't quite so argumentative with his teacher. But his handwriting was still illegible, he still wasn't doing homework, and his parents were still convinced that only half of his problem was being tackled. That's when they came to see me.

Even without testing, I could see the discrepancies in Doug's functioning and the reason for his frustration. He might always have a problem with writing, but there were many ways of getting around this. He could use a tape recorder, learn to type, and work on his handwriting. In the meantime, though, he needed help just as much as any other child with learning differences. Because he was so bright, no one believed he really had a problem and everyone expected more of him than he could deliver. He also expected too much of himself. When he couldn't perform well, he would freeze—and then quit.

Doug needed understanding and a chance to excel instead of always being penalized for his disabilities. To improve his self-esteem, others had to recognize his outstanding abilities instead of dwelling on his lack of performance. Doug was most definitely a youngster who belonged with the brightest kids in the mainstream of education but he needed remedial work, therapy, and a support system—all at the same time. With all three, there could be optimism about his future.

With gifted youngsters, particularly, things tend to come together more quickly with appropriate help. They usually make excellent progress because of their sensitivity and advanced level of understanding. Doug certainly did. The change after six months of intensive work on his writing was amazing. He also learned to use the typewriter for homework assignments—or enlist his mother's cooperation as "secretary." I joked with him that he could always turn to medicine as a profession, since most doctors don't write so legibly either.

Leonardo da Vinci had a learning disability—and certainly was gifted. So was my friend Andy. He would come home from school every day and immediately closet himself in his room with paper and crayons. Hours later, he would come down to dinner, sit silently at the table, and then return to his hideaway. His parents appreciated his creativity but were distressed that he spent so much time alone and never played outside. Their efforts to bring him into family life were for naught, though; he seemed to be in a world of his own.

Andy's third-grade teacher wasn't so worried about his lack of participation in class; she was annoyed by his daydreaming and his inattention. He sat at his desk, either drawing pictures or staring out the window. When she did get his

attention, he would need a full briefing on what the assignment was. Andy was "out of it" wherever he was.

Andy had trouble talking as well as listening in class. He
couldn't seem to find words to express himself and he didn't
often try. His teacher pointed this out to his parents who had
not realized how profound his problems were. It was true
that he had been a late talker, but when he did speak, he
could usually make himself understood. His parents had
assumed that he was just a quiet, not-very-verbal child, who
perhaps, like many creative children, needed time to himself.
They were right in feeling that being alone should not always
be confused with being lonely. Still, I felt it would not do to
simply dismiss his problem with an "Oh, well, it's just his
artistic nature." Andy still had to live much of his life in the
real world of parents, teachers, and peers—and he wasn't
making it there.

As I got to know Andy better, he admitted that he was
unhappy because he had no friends. At school he was
laughed at and sometimes called "sissy" or "gay." As it
happened, he wasn't a bad athlete, but he was afraid to
chance the rebuffs on the playground, so he opted to stay in
for recess and draw. That was his talent and it was also his
escape. But each day his loneliness grew and his aggressive
fantasies along with it. His pictures of space wars and weapons of destruction gave evidence of his angry inner life.

I tried to help Andy's teacher appreciate his language
problems as well as his artistic gifts. Andy started language
therapy in school, and at the same time his teacher began to
capitalize on his talent. When she did that, the third-grade
class had the best scenery in the school for its play, and the
halls outside the classroom were filled with Andy's creations.
Gradually, he began to find a place for himself—important
for all children, but perhaps harder to find when one is gifted
and LD.

The academically gifted child is perhaps hardest to picture
as LD. It is a truism, though, that academic talent does not

ensure success in school. When a youngster without serious emotional problems is impulsive, unaware of others around him, and can't read the signals in life the way others do, his primary learning disability is social. He may be on such a different wavelength that he is alienated from all.

Sam, at eleven, was truly socially disabled. He had been skipped in first grade because he was reading so well. That hadn't helped him socially since he was smaller and younger than everyone else. He was a brilliant but "dumb" boy who collected enemies the way other people collect stamps. He didn't perceive his effect on others or do what was expected. He actually seemed to look for rejection—and he got it. Everything he did set him up as a target for ridicule. He reminded me of the little boy in the story of Epaminondas whose mother always said in frustration, "You just don't have the sense you were born with." Like the storybook character, Sam could be counted on to try to do the right thing—but always at the wrong time! His inner clock always seemed out of whack.

Sam was so unaware of the feelings of others that he'd be the first to laugh if someone tripped and fell; yet, he would never knowingly hurt anyone himself and he was particularly gentle with younger or handicapped children. He was also an impulsive "blurter" who said whatever he was thinking—which was usually inappropriate or uncalled-for. One day after school, he got into his car with a new friend and burst out, "Mom, this is Ralph. He's adopted."

Ralph became his only friend that year and when he moved away, Sam was depressed for weeks. He was an only child with no one at home to fight with or learn from, and he was in such trouble with his peers that when he invited the boys in the neighborhood to his birthday party, no one showed up. His parents were devastated, perhaps even more than Sam.

Only with adults did his real personality come through. He could be charming and witty, with intelligence enough to hold his own in a serious conversation. He loved being with his parents' friends and they enjoyed his company. He told me, "I always get along better with older people. I guess I'm an elitist."

Teachers, too, appreciated Sam during class discussions, except when he interrupted or shouted out impulsively. But when it was time to get out papers and books, he seemed the center of a small hurricane. Again, he invited laughter and jeers from the class. His desk was a mess, he was rarely prepared for tests (although he usually did well), and he never knew when an assignment was due. This disorganization was part of his learning disability too.

Sam was not only disorganized at school; he was also absent-minded at home. In one year, he had lost four jackets and thirteen gloves—all right hands. His mother also complained that it was a full-time job to keep Sam occupied at home. He was easily bored; he had no friends and was particular about the TV programs he watched. He was even ultra-picky about books and so did little reading for pleasure. His parents told me they found it hard to appreciate his high IQ when living with him was so difficult. For him, "LD" stood for "living disabilities."

Both the school and Sam's parents were determined to find a way to motivate and organize him. Even Sam said, "I know I need structure. Maybe someone could help me get my act together." His parents hired a tutor who, merely by organizing Sam's notebook, helped him feel more in control. They went on from there to organize homework and study time.

The next step was to find outlets that were enriching enough to capture Sam's imagination. A bright child with social problems is more likely to respond to other children who share his abilities and ideas. A Saturday morning science club at the local high school sounded like a logical choice, even if most of the boys were older. Sam loved fooling around with test tubes and Bunsen burners with his lab partner, a gifted boy from another school. Their morning sessions eventually evolved into lunch dates after the club meetings.

Most of all, Sam needed to work on his social perception. Youngsters with learning differences probably learn best from their peers—but only in non-threatening situations. I had a boys' group and Sam seemed a logical addition. I hoped the other youngsters could accomplish what Sam's parents and teachers could not. He had to learn a great deal more about his impact on others—and how to be tactful—before he could become part of any social scene. This turned out to be the most difficult aspect of Sam's treatment. He was so uncomfortable in the company of boys his age that he always managed to do and say the wrong thing. It took a long time for him to relax enough to join the others in activities and become more aware of appropriate behavior. I doubt that Sam will ever be an exceptionally tuned-in, sensitive friend but perhaps with successful experiences in other areas of his life, he will find companionship.

Much has been said about whether gifted youngsters are more or less popular than their peers who are not exceptional. While it is impossible to generalize about the popularity of any group as a whole, the acceptance of gifted children appears to be related to their skill at social interaction, the degree and type of their giftedness, and the availability of at least a few exceptionally able peers for companionship.

Most brilliant children tend to assess their own behavior fairly accurately, and predict their social status as well as that of their peers. This reflects their advanced social perception and comprehension. For the youngsters I have talked about, though, this was not necessarily the case. They were socially inept, while performing in other areas with the most advanced. This can be a special kind of burden—for the children and for those responsible for them. One of the most neglected areas in working with gifted LD youngsters is that of counseling for their parents. Parents of exceptional children frequently need help to really come to terms with their children's problems as well as their potential.

To make sure that the gifted LD child is given the opportunity to achieve his potential, careful diagnosis and planning are important. Early intervention can result in significant improvement in learning, but attention must also be paid to the social adjustment of these children. They need not be isolated from their peers just because they are gifted, LD —or both.

chapter
7

GETTING TOGETHER
IN GROUPS

Tony's mother, always on the lookout for ways to help her son, called me one evening with an interesting idea. She wondered if I had ever thought of starting a group for LD youngsters with social problems. Tony was having a hard time socially and she had just learned that her friend's son, Richard, was too. Both boys had learning disabilities and were making progress with the remedial help offered in school. Still, their lack of companionship continued to frustrate both families.

The idea of a group sounded like it might work and I enlisted the help of Bill Tarplin, a well-trained and skilled group therapist who was chief of social services for children at a nearby hospital.

In thinking of ways to organize the group, Bill and I decided to keep it small because youngsters with learning differences tend to become overstimulated in a crowd. We also limited it to boys, partly because it was the parents of boys who volunteered as soon as the idea was mentioned. Within a week, we had our group: five boys, nine to eleven-and-a-half years of age.

One of the principles of group therapy is that members can help each other because of their similar problems and concerns. Our youngsters had a double bond from the start— their learning problems and their lack of friends. Most of them came from different school districts, which was a plus in that academic and social competition was minimized. Only Tony and Richard had known each other before.

We hoped that the boys would gain from the group perspective and insight into their own behavior, perhaps for the first time. We also hoped that what happened in the group would be transferred to home, school, and playground. Because we would not be able to observe the boys outside of the group, we would rely on their parents and teachers to keep us informed. Finally, we hoped the group would provide some companionship and interaction with peers in a safe, uncritical place. Social learning is impossible in a vacuum and these boys apparently spent much of their leisure time alone. With the group, at least they could be assured of one time a week when they would be with others their age for social purposes.

Until this group formed, I wasn't sure why these attractive, nice kids didn't have friends, but after three or four meetings of the group, the problem became quite clear.

One of the boys, Tony, revealed some of the characteristics of LD children that affect their social relationships. First was his immaturity: he seemed much younger than boys of his age, physically and in the quality of his language. He also seemed unable to understand what was happening outside his own immediate world. He had a very short attention span and found it difficult to stay with a subject for any length of time. We could count on his becoming giggly and silly before the end of any discussion or activity. We even lost him in the middle of juice and cookies!

Richard was quite the opposite of Tony, physically. He was the largest in the group and had been accustomed to using his fists to assert himself. He was the class bully to such an extent that his strength had even begun to frighten *him*. He was trying hard to control himself that year but he still had a vicious tongue which he used freely to put others down. While Richard had not learned to read until fourth grade, he was suddenly doing better in sixth. Only his problems with math and his social disabilities remained.

Richard craved attention in the group and loved to monopolize the conversation. He was the group know-it-all, our self-appointed resident expert, who boasted about his prowess in everything. He really couldn't see that he was being offensive when he played the game of one-upmanship.

Insensitivity is another characteristic typical of youngsters with learning problems and it did alienate Richard until we began to point it out to him. One of us would occasionally say, "It's very hard for you to admit that anyone else knows anything, isn't it? You need to have a monopoly on being smart." But when Lance, the meekest in the group, said, "Shut up, Richard, you don't know everything about everything. Can't you see I was talking?" we knew something important was happening for both boys.

Lance was generally mild, sensitive and shadowy. He was rarely definite about anything. He had a nervous twitch which usually signaled that he had something to say but was afraid his listeners would disappear unless he spoke quickly. He was obviously trying to please, but was so nervous about it that it was easy to see why he was rejected. His vulnerability made him the perfect scapegoat. Surprisingly, though, he was not picked on when he was with us. In time, Lance developed strength, at least in the group.

Alan was small, wiry, and hyperactive. He was constantly chewing on his collar or shoelaces, and playing with everything in sight. He moved and talked constantly, interrupting every conversation with an irrelevant but self-centered comment. His egocentricity and impulsiveness were apparent. Of all the boys, Alan was the only one who seemed not to care that he didn't have friends. It didn't even seem to bother him when he was ignored.

By the end of the year, it was apparent that Alan's problems went deeper than his social disabilities. After much deliberation, Bill and I recommended individual psychotherapy rather than his continuing in the group. Actually, both forms of treatment might have been appropriate, but his parents were already burdened with a hectic schedule and had to choose one or the other.

The fifth boy was Herbert, a little old man, joyless and

often sarcastic. We decided that he was somewhat less biting than his father only because he had had fewer years of practice. He saw himself as a younger version of his father who also greeted everything with a sneer. This attitude tended to disappear over time, though, and Herbert became more spontaneous in the group. He even became babyish at times, teasing the other boys and disrupting their games. The boys sometimes asked why Herbert was acting that way (they called it "spazzed"), but they seemed to understand that it was the first time he felt comfortable enough to "be himself."

What all the boys shared, whatever their individual problem, was the feeling one of them expressed at our very first meeting: "I guess I'm here because I don't have enough friends."

Two themes dominated that first session and were prominent in many subsequent meetings. The first was all the "weirdos" the boys knew or had known. The other topic that developed revolved around all the dangerous adventures they had had, including lighting matches, climbing on roofs, and playing with firecrackers. The two themes seemed significant in combination. The first reflected the boys' obvious feelings about themselves as being different and perhaps even "weird" in terms of their learning disabilities. It was apparently easier for them to talk about others rather than themselves. The second theme had to do with their wish to be brave. They would have loved to be thought of as daring and carefree instead of weak and ineffectual, as they perceived themselves.

The activities of the group were as revealing as the discussions. Watching the boys play and compete with one another provided new insights. A game of checkers between Lance and Richard revealed that each boy had his own style, consistent with his personality. Lance kept his men out of the line of fire, moving from the back rows as little as possible. Bright as he was, he could not begin to plan a strategy, or even see how his piece had been jumped. His spatial problems were as obvious as his need to protect himself from aggression.

Richard, on the other hand, always aggressive, pushed his men forward impulsively and without fear. He didn't wince when his pieces were captured but he cheated whenever he could. He argued vociferously, and made up his own rules as he went along. It was one of the funniest non-games I'd ever seen. Richard claimed victory to the end with only a piece left, while Lance shouted, "This is the best game I ever played, 'cause I never won before."

One of the most common themes of discussion among the boys had to do with being teased by peers, particularly about their lack of athletic ability. No one had the answer but they all had ideas about what to do. Lance said, "If you sock 'em, they'll stop teasing," but he readily admitted that he had never tried this approach; he was too afraid of the "bullies." Once, when we were alone, he wrote this paragraph:

> All Bullies are the same no matter what they do. One is they will pretend to teese you and they don't mean it. Two is sometimes they will stick up for you if Big Bullies push you around. Three is if they know you will fight back they will stop.

Richard, usually aggressive, said, "Try ignoring them. Just walk away and they'll stop bothering you." It was apparent, though, that he never could be that "cool." His advice was in the "do as I say and not as I do" department. Then, someone else, having possibly picked up some techniques from us, offered, "Why don't you just talk to them? Maybe they don't know how you feel when you're teased." Dead silence followed that bit of wisdom.

While no one strategy seemed appropriate or effective for every boy, we found that role playing taught the boys to handle their oppressors somewhat better, each in his own style. Perhaps, though, they gained most from the recognition that they were not the only victims in the world: others were picked on too.

During the first two years of the group these youngsters

grew and changed, possibly because they had peers to talk to, the uncritical and accepting attitude of adults, and the use of activities as a means of building confidence. At one meeting, Lance said, "I like coming to the group because it's the only place I never get yelled at." Richard claimed the group helped him gain "self-control and friends," and Tony said, "I'm learning how to talk about all the things that bug me."

We also heard from parents that the boys seemed to be getting along better outside the group: they each had a good summer and, for three of them, even camp experiences were positive for the first time.

A year after the boys' group began, I started a group for five pre-adolescent girls, ages ten to twelve. As with the boys' group, I met first with the parents, who were vocal about their objectives and hopes for their daughters. One father said, "Reading is not my daughter's main difficulty. Confidence in herself is." A mother said, "I can tell her something ten times and she won't listen, but if a friend says so, she will." Still another plaintively wished to go back to being "just a mother." She was tired, she said, of being her daughter's "best and only friend."

The format or plan for the sessions was very much the same as for the boys' group. Choice of activity was decided by the girls, sometimes in advance, often on the spur of the moment. We spent the first part of each session catching up with one another in my office. We could then move to the kitchen for cooking or the playroom for shuffleboard, ping-pong, or jewelry-making. The girls also enjoyed card games and charades.

The issues that concerned the girls most were different from the boys. One basic concern among the girls was the theme of family relationships, particularly problems with brothers. As an aside, it was interesting that all of the girls had at least one brother and none had a sister. Perhaps they related to one another quickly because of this common bond —or common enemy. As we followed the thread of brother-sister relationships, we heard the usual complaints about teasing and domination. These girls, though, seemed to feel very much like second-class citizens, even if the much maligned brother was only five years old. They all felt strongly that their brothers were more competent and got more attention than they did.

Another common theme revolved around the age-old problems of assuming responsibility for household chores and homework. Most of the girls mentioned that it was hard for them to get organized. They felt their parents intruded too much but they were willing to admit that they usually needed prodding to get things done on time. Once, one girl made the comment that her mother blamed everything on her learning disability, using it to account for *all* her behavior. She felt this was unfair.

The girls were at very different stages of development when it came to boy/girl relationships. Perhaps there was even more variability than would be found among youngsters without LD problems. Two of them seemed not at all interested in the opposite sex, and others were precocious and developed. Their perceptions were a bit unrealistic, though, and their fantasies overly ripe. One girl, in particular, saw herself as twelve going on twenty-two. She wished the boys would think of her as gorgeous rather than peculiar.

Whenever we were engaged in serious talk about growing up, one member or another would eventually "blow." It seemed as if the girls could only deal with the topic of their budding maturity for a limited time without reverting to a pointless "bathroom joke," some gruesome black humor, or regression to a nursery school kind of game. After one particularly "hot" moment, one girl actually suggested that we play ring-around-a-rosy. None of the other girls thought this was strange, and play it we did!

All the girls felt left out—or even scapegoated—by the "in" group at school. We began to talk about the qualities that might encourage social acceptance or the lack of it. Again, many of these reflected the girls' learning problems.

One might lack empathy, while another might talk too much or act so babyish she didn't fit in. The beginnings of self-awareness were necessary before changes could take place. One girl learned to ask for a "high-sign" when she was talking too much. Another became more aware of her appearance and had her hair cut; she became less intrusive as well.

"Rap sessions" also seemed helpful. Each girl in the group would tell the others how she felt about them, gently and without rancor. One-liners like, "You sure do talk a lot," "Why do you always get silly when you don't win," or "You giggle more than anybody," seemed to have been accepted comfortably.

The girls set their own rules for "rapping." Each would name one strong point and one fault for each girl. When we began, I noticed that their comments were not cruel. Some of the girls found it hard to do, though, while others could be more direct. If we were to characterize the girls' behavior, it was varied; at times babyish and regressed, at other times remarkably insightful, but usually caring and supportive of one another.

From my experience with groups, it seems apparent that a discussion-activity model can be an effective form of treatment for LD children with social problems from the time they are quite young through adolesence. (LD adults can benefit, too.) Regardless of age, people with learning problems can accept reactions and suggestions from one another in a group. Perhaps because they share similar concerns and experiences, they are able to communicate. And most important, they do seem able to modify their behavior, first within the group and then outside. The result is improved social competence and greater self-esteem.

chapter
8

LEARNING PROBLEMS—
AND PIMPLES TOO!

The need for social acceptance has been called the engine
that drives the behavior of most teenagers. It will not surprise
any parent to hear that what Danny's friends think of him
is more important to him at the age of fifteen than how he
is doing in school. The adolescent years are the conforming
years—not necessarily to parental values but to the peer
group. This is the time when young people normally turn
from parents toward peers for companionship and a sharing
of feelings.

Young people who have grown up with learning disabilities usually have a very hard time. If they haven't developed
appropriate behavior and social judgment, they probably
don't have friends and are not accepted socially. Their un-
resolved problems of short attention span, poor memory,
hyperactivity, and immaturity may contribute to their social
problems. By the time they reach adolescence, they are unable to keep pace with the increasing social demands. Peer
pressure, coupled with their wish to experiment with adult
behavior they don't fully understand, can make this a haz-
ardous time. These are the youngsters who seem to be in
culture shock in their own culture.

Patti is only one of many children I have known who never
seemed to understand the social scene. She always had problems with her contemporaries, but usually got along better
with younger children. When she changed schools in ninth

grade, she welcomed the opportunity to start over and make new friends. But her enthusiasm was quickly dashed. She seemed to have nothing in common with the kids in her new school who were involved in clothes, boys, and "pot." Patti wasn't nearly ready for these activities but, at the same time, she wanted desperately to fit in. She was tempted to join the others, although she was scared. No one even gave her the chance, though, since she was considered "such a creep."

Patti seemed to have some insight into her problems for one day she told me, "I'm not a follower because I think for myself, but I'm not a leader because I don't have enough self-confidence."

I didn't realize how bad things were until Patti's mother called me in a panic. Apparently Patti had been cutting classes for weeks. When confronted, she admitted that she couldn't face going to most of them. Her teachers were "boring," the work was "hard," and most of all, the kids gave her "a pain." She was feeling completely friendless and alone at school.

The LD teenager is probably even more vulnerable to rejection than younger children. The persistent lack of peer acceptance through the years slowly erodes an already fragile ego. The history of failure contributes to the feeling "I can't do anything right." The adolescent who tends to deprecate himself anyway may come to see his whole life as a series of mistakes and misfortunes. "How could I be so stupid?" and "Why do I always bomb with kids?" are familiar themes.

The bleakness of existence for these young people may eventually lead to even more serious consequences. In the past few years, much has been written about adolescent rebellion and delinquency, depression and suicide. While these problems are certainly not confined to the LD population, for the adolescent with social disabilities there may well be a close connection. It is little wonder that concern about the social adjustment of LD adolescents is growing. How to help them survive this period and come out of it with a positive identity of their own is a challenge for parents and professionals alike.

I can remember worrying about Jack who, at fifteen, still had residual learning disabilities. He had been in special classes and resource rooms until he got to high school. Then, because he was tired of feeling "different" (and the program wasn't particularly good anyway), he was put in a regular class. But he fared no better socially than academically. He was drowning in the mainstream.

Jack was small, late to mature physically (a distinct disadvantage for boys in our society), and impetuous. He was completely unaware of how he came across to others and tried to act important, using foul and provocative language. This did not appeal to the group of boys he wanted to join, though, and he was constantly rebuffed. But his behavior did make him attractive to the *least* desirable kids in school—the "hoods," as they were called.

Jack became involved in situations that he knew were dangerous, yet he was so eager to be part of the crowd that he didn't worry while he was with them. But afterwards, he told me, he'd "break into a cold sweat" at the thought of getting caught. Petty vandalism in the school, drinking, smoking, and truancy were all part of Jack's new world.

Not all aberrant behavior in adolescence is necessarily part of an LD syndrome the way it probably was for Jack. Adolescents experiment: the boy who violates social taboos may be trying so hard to prove himself worthy of a new clique that he temporarily loses his perspective. He may settle down fairly quickly after that.

For the young person who is impetuous and insecure to begin with, though, the "acting out" crowd is a natural affiliation. Jack, a decent boy with basically good instincts, had gotten himself in a bind that could have affected him for the rest of his life. He was testing the limits, as so many adolescents do, particularly when they are frustrated in school.

Fortunately, Jack's parents cared enough to intervene. They were kept constantly on edge, but recognizing the rebelliousness of his nature—and of his age—they walked the necessary tightrope. They understood they couldn't stand by passively watching Jack get into trouble, but neither could they impose their will too arbitrarily. Merely telling Jack to stop what he was doing or "grounding" him probably wouldn't have worked. In fact, when they tried to talk to him, Jack became defensive, insisting that he could handle his own life.

His parents and an interested school counselor guided him into more constructive activities after school that kept him involved with suitable companions. Jack didn't like sports, but he did become interested in photography and chess. He was also invited to join the stage crew at his high school and kept busy with school plays. Finally, he was given more tutorial help so he could pass his courses.

One of Jack's friends, though, had not been so lucky. Doug's learning disabilities had been recognized but not attended to. He attended a large urban school and had been promoted each year, though he still couldn't read. His father was distant and uninvolved, his mother domineering, and he never got along with either one very well. In the early years, Doug had been quiet and unobtrusive. As he grew, his passive personality made him a follower who was easily influenced. He seemed to have no identity of his own but took on the characteristics of anyone he was with.

In adolescence, he became part of the neighborhood gang that was involved in delinquent activities and drugs. At first, Doug only took "uppers" when he felt depressed, but that condition must have occurred more and more because he was obviously addicted by the time he was sixteen. He began stealing from his mother's purse and anyone else's that was lying around, but even that didn't provide enough money to support his habit. Eventually, he was expelled from school after having been caught dealing drugs.

Doug was remanded to a drug rehabilitation program where, for the first time, he had family therapy, as well as group therapy—and his learning disabilities were dealt with. Most of his teachers were former addicts themselves, now dedicated to helping others to a better life. They taught

Doug, and they influenced him. Because of them, he eventually did pass the high school equivalency exam and could make plans for his future.

Doug was one of the lucky ones. Many, many youngsters, even those who enter therapy groups, are lost each year to a decent life. Parents who think their LD youngsters may be taking drugs or are involved in dangerous or illegal activities should deal with the problems head on. Denying, making excuses, or being afraid to confront a rebellious teenager is counterproductive. An angry youngster, determined to keep his parents at arm's length, can be a tough adversary, but a strong parental voice is called for.

It has long been thought, though perhaps not proved, that many young drug addicts and juvenile delinquents have learning disabilities. The failure and frustration at school have drawn them into troubled, antisocial, and delinquent behavior. They seek peer acceptance wherever they can find it—and mostly it is from those with similar problems. Such young people reinforce each other's bad habits. Because of their impulsive behavior and lack of judgment, they take dares and experiment more readily, without considering the consequences. Recent research shows a very high incidence of learning disabilities among young people in correctional institutions.*

It is encouraging, though, that drug rehabilitation programs as well as the juvenile court system today recognize the link between "LD" and "JD." Many facilities are providing therapy and training in life skills for this population. Those in charge hope that this will turn the young people around and reduce the amount of recidivism.

Not all adolescent experimentation involves youngsters in conflict with the law. In today's fast-moving and stimulating society, there are many temptations to try all kinds of adult

*"Report from Closer Look." Washington, D.C.: Closer Look, Fall 1980, p. 7.

roles too soon. Teenagers, bombarded by the media, are told that sex is the key to fulfillment and success. Without a boyfriend, say the latest records and magazines, no girl's life is complete. The assumption is made that every nymphet beyond the age of ten knows the facts of life; and indeed, many of them do. They have undoubtedly learned more from their pals than from their parents. For the LD adolescents, however, who have no companions with whom to share secrets and confidences, knowledge of sexual matters can be sadly lacking. And even what they have heard may not have been fully understood.

One unsophisticated fifteen-year-old I worked with thought she knew it all. When we read about the development of the fetus for a science assignment, she seemed to have fairly accurate information. I was quickly disabused, however, when she told me with assurance that a pregnant woman had to eat carefully since what she ate went "right to the baby's mouth through the tube." I had to laugh as I pictured an embryo eating a Big Mac second-hand.

This girl had had intimate relations with boys without any knowledge of contraception. Because she was so hungry for affection, she would do anything. Premature sexual activity can be a consequence of loneliness as well as the ingenuousness of adolescent girls with learning disabilities. They may be less mature—and more easily persuaded to put aside the standards they may have been brought up to live by. Once they have done that, they have probably also shut off communication with their parents. Thus ends their sex education and guidance from home.

Sex education in most schools is poor and does not provide nearly enough of the kind of information these young people need. Involvement with sex is so interwoven with emotions that the customary class lectures and self-conscious discussions are simply too superficial. And besides, youngsters with learning disabilities may require far more concrete and graphic presentations than many local school boards deem appropriate.

Parents too, on the whole, do an inadequate job of preparing their children to accept and deal sensibly and happily with their sexuality. An older friend or physician may be able to convey more information—if the LD teenager wants to hear it. If not, a trained counselor should be asked to work with the child. Another source of sex information might be a guidance group. Whoever does the job, though, should understand that sex cannot be isolated from the issues of loneliness, growing up, and the social situations most teenagers are concerned with. They should all be part of the agenda.

In contrast with those who are overstimulated in adolescence, some young people grow up naïve and fearful of their burgeoning sexuality. They are not ready for even the most ordinary boy-girl experiences. They adopt a Peter Pan attitude, unwilling to grow up; they flee from any close relationship. This sets these teenagers apart even more from the typical adolescents who are willing, or even eager, to move toward adulthood. I've seen young people withdraw more and more until they have no outside interests or involvement at all. They come straight home from school to watch soap operas on TV and spend the rest of the day fulfilling their fantasies in front of the "tube."

Roberta, a girl with learning disabilities, isolated herself this way. She wanted to turn down an invitation to a graduation party. She told me she really wished she could go, knowing that "normal kids" would be there, but she was afraid she wouldn't know what to say to them. She only felt comfortable with her friends from the special classes in high school.

I decided it was about time to introduce Roberta to society at large. We rehearsed conversations that might take place at a party and talked about how she could refuse a "joint" or a drink if offered one. It took several sessions, but she finally did agree to go to the party, knowing she could leave if she felt too uncomfortable.

Adolescents so out of synch with their age group are likely to resort to unproductive ways of coping. These might be called the "Adolescent Three Fs": Fight, Flee, or Follow. Jack fought, Doug followed, while Roberta fled. One of the more drastic flights, perhaps, is escape into one of the cults. These groups have particular appeal for the socially unaccepted, unattractive teenagers who feel lost and alone. Many such young people are learning-disabled. The youngsters must have that searching look, too, for they seem to be easily found by those who prey on susceptible teenagers. Parents today have legitimate fears about the exploitation of their children by those who proselytize for cults. While there are no pat ways to prevent this from happening, parents cannot afford to ignore how their youngsters are feeling. Unhappiness is usually fairly transparent, and that is what makes young people vulnerable to the charismatic qualities of cult leaders.

Perhaps knowing that so many youngsters do get into difficulty in adolescence, parents, too, become more anxious during this period. They are aware that adolescence can sometimes turn even the most "together" kid into a distant, sullen stranger. As one mother complained, "Where did my sweet little girl go? I don't recognize this cranky, defiant person I'm living with. We fight all the time these days." This is certainly not true for all adolescents, but many do become moody during this time.

If children who have had a good relationship with their parents—and no prior problems—can change, how much more difficult it must be for the adolescent who trails a history of learning disabilities. One girl I had been seeing was quite handicapped, and as a teenager had to be taught to handle money, to travel by herself, and to make her own arrangements with friends. There was so much for her to master that it took a long time before she could assert any independence at all. Her mother became so alarmed at the thought of what her daughter might do once she achieved independence that she tightened the parental controls rather than loosening them, as I was encouraging her to do. Her daughter interpreted this as mistrust and became terribly resentful. The tension at home built up until the daughter stopped speaking to her mother and was threatening to run away. While I could understand this mother's anxiety, I also believed that the girl was ready for more freedom and responsibility.

Some parents of LD children never do learn to trust their youngsters. They worry that because of their learning disabilities, they won't exercise good judgment and self-control. A friend of mine even went to the extreme of reading her daughter's diary. She was so concerned about what her daughter was doing that she invaded her privacy. Adolescence is a time when young people need to have some secrets from their parents. That is the beginning of separation and growing up. This mother found it threatening to be excluded from her daughter's confidence, but she endangered their relationship by her lack of faith. It is understandable that parents may want to know more than they are told by their children, but they, too, need to exercise self-control. They can no longer expect their offspring to be completely under their wings, and they have to come to terms with the new arrangement.

Just because parents are not privy to all the facts does not mean they must abdicate their responsibility to guide their teenagers. Parents should make the attempt to talk and keep the lines of communication open, even if they're not sure they are heard. They may have to meet their children *more* than halfway, particularly if there is no peer group available to act as a sounding board. Admittedly, this is hard to do when you are angry or feel out of touch with your own child. It can be a long, tiring road through adolescence for parents of LD youngsters.

The mother of fifteen-year-old Betsy called me one day, saying that she and her daughter were going to "kill each other" if something didn't change. She and her husband had provided years of special schools, tutors, and a lot of loving care for Betsy. They had done all they could to support her and they had expected that by now things would be easier for all of them. But Betsy was presenting more problems than ever. She was putting on too much weight, antagonizing everyone at home, and her room was "an absolute pigsty." Betsy's mother said she was so angry with her that there was "nothing to praise, ever." She was also worried that Betsy was taking two steps backward for every step forward she had made when she was younger.

The summer was looming ahead with some additional problems. Betsy had refused to go back to camp, saying she was "too old" and "hated it." Betsy's mother envisioned a long, difficult summer with Betsy at home. Fortunately, we were able to find a travel program that was geared to the needs of LD teenagers. This meant a slightly slower pace and some academic instruction along the way. Learning to take care of belongings, budgeting spending money, and seeing new places are obvious advantages to this kind of summer. The social growth that occurs may be less noticeable, perhaps, but a group of peers can be just what an isolated, lonely teenager needs. Needless to say, the trip also had the advantage of providing a respite for Betsy's mother. That was not the summer they should spend together.

Parental worries may increase as teenagers get older and the issues of late-night hours and driving arise. The LD youngsters with a poor sense of time and/or the desire to defy authority can cause many sleepless nights when they don't check in on time. And if they have just learned to handle the family car after failing the driving test three times, a lot of gray hair may result. Some guidelines are important, but risks do have to be taken if teenagers are ever going to graduate from home.

LD or not, adolescents worry about peer relations, employment, sex, and possibly marriage, but the outcome may be more in doubt for those with learning problems. Finding their own identity and a direction for the future is a persistent concern, particularly for those who feel different. Unable to achieve independence and self-reliance by themselves, LD adolescents may continue to need many of the same resources they have had all along: family support, school programs, and opportunities for peer interaction.

Perhaps the first thing for parents to realize is that they have only a limited role at this stage in their children's lives. They may have to back off considerably, even though their adolescent still has a long way to go to reach maturity. If, like Betsy's parents, they find themselves distraught and fed up, this may be the right time to ask for outside help. They may need to share the burden they have been carrying alone and get some advice on how to live more comfortably with their LD teenagers.

There are many options available within the counseling field. Individual therapy, family counseling, and group discussion are all viable alternatives. Jo, one of the teenagers I had seen for a long time, summarized her treatment in the following way: "I didn't feel I belonged because I was so different, with my learning problems and all. I didn't feel socially acceptable, but I found that the only person who felt this way was me. When I worked on my problems, it really made a difference. A good attitude counts for a lot. I feel better now that I'm not copping out."

One of the best things Jo had done, in addition to working on her problems, was to take a two-week backpacking trip in the summer with a group of teenagers. It had taken months to convince her to go, but she finally mustered the courage. It was her first experience living with others her age and she didn't fail as she had feared. She actually got along well with the girls, which gave her self-confidence. She particularly liked one of the group leaders on the trip, who became her role model. Finding someone to admire and emulate is probably one of the most effective ways for teenagers to learn how successful people get along.

Youngsters with learning problems frequently cannot learn from verbal explanation alone. They may think too slowly and concretely to understand what is being said, so they need to copy what they see and hear. One of my students said she used to think of her calm, soft-spoken aunt whenever she got into a shouting match with her friends. Emulating her aunt helped her change her own tone of voice and cool down a bit.

One of the things I've noticed about teenagers who don't feel good about themselves is that they don't look so good either. They are often unkempt and ill-clad, adolescent styles notwithstanding. Their messiness and out-of-mode dress make them even more outcast socially. When I have found legitimate reasons to compliment them (clean fingernails, a haircut, or "unholey" jeans), I have noticed that matching socks or a clean shirt may appear at our next meeting. Compliments rather than criticism have a snowball effect. Grooming may sound like an unimportant issue on which to focus, but it may be one more reason an LD teenager stands out from the crowd. He may not even be aware of how he looks—unless his classmates tell him.

In high school, young people are quick to spot those who don't fit in, even academically. Being in "slow" classes and resource rooms, while necessary, is enough to set an LD student apart. Classmates know—and comment on—who is taking what subject and why. I remember the day one of my students was strolling down the hall with a boy who asked what English class she was in. When Nancy told him, he scoffed, "Are you kidding? I took that three years ago. What's the matter with you?" Nancy was devastated and made a beeline for the Rap Room, so-called in her school. "I want to be where I'm not singled out," she cried to the first person she saw.

Unfortunate as the experience was, at least she had a haven at school—and peer counselors to listen to her. They were students who had taken a training course in human relations and volunteered to help other students. There may not be too many high schools across the country that provide rap rooms and peer counseling, but what a good idea it is! The combination of active listening and a climate of warmth builds trust and self-esteem.

At the end of the year, Nancy's parents and her advisor agreed, though, that the school's academic program was just too much for her. Since she wasn't planning to go on to college anyway, the subjects with which she was struggling were not even practical. Nancy thought she might like hair-dressing, so she was directed to the cosmetology program in a nearby community. She was excited at the prospect of being trained for a job instead of taking courses she would never use—and which she found so difficult. This would not mean that she was severing all ties with her high school, though. Her program would still include the learning center, typing, and gym. (A well-planned physical education class, in partic-ular, can do a lot to foster social skills.)

Soon after school started in September, Nancy took the special bus to the cosmetology class. She said she could tell right away that she was "the only one with learning disabili-ties." (She had always had a sixth sense about who had problems like hers—and she gravitated to them.)

For the first couple of days, all went well—until the text-books were given out. She took one look at the small print, the technical vocabulary, and the chapter tests and "almost died," to use her words. This was going to be even harder than algebra! And sure enough, when everyone settled down to read Chapter I, Nancy was stuck. She said she knew everyone was looking at her when she groaned, wondering what was wrong. They obviously didn't know she had a reading problem.

Then and there, Nancy said she decided to come to her own defense. She asked the teacher if she would please talk to the class about her problems. To avoid embarrassment, Nancy left the room while her teacher tried to explain what the trouble was.

What happened next was unplanned but fortuitous. When she saw me later that day, Nancy reported that when she had reentered the room, one of the girls still had some questions. Nancy said she wouldn't mind answering them, and for the next half hour the class discussed learning disabilities. Nancy was asked how long she had had a learning disability, what it really meant, and whether it would go away.

Nancy explained to the class that she had always had trouble in school and she couldn't read or spell as well as the others. She also needed much more time to get work done. Then she added, "I don't have a lot of friends as I wish I did, and most of my friends have a learning disability of some kind too." Nancy went on to say that if she had one wish, it would be "not to have a learning disability for one whole day—twenty-four hours' worth."

During that year, Nancy's teacher found many ways to modify the course for her. She got a tape recording of the textbook, gave Nancy the tests orally, and found out that she could have both a reader and a scribe for the written state licensing exam when the time came.

Nancy was in the forefront of a new look to vocational education. Traditionally, job training has been predominantly for the non-handicapped student and is often just as difficult as regular academic programs. Maybe that's why there are so few people with learning disabilities enrolled in occupational education courses. While there are a few excellent ones dotted around the country that serve those with learning problems, the majority of programs are based on old, worn-out trade school stereotypes. They make little use of what has been learned in special education.

What is needed is a team effort between special educators concerned with the needs of young people and the professionals who teach vocational courses. Vocational education is a viable alternative to an academic high school program for many LD students who need a course of study combining literacy and basic job skills. The curriculum should dovetail academic skills, career training, and hands-on experience. Then education will no longer be the dead end it has been for so many LD students.

While appropriate schooling is crucial, in the end what count are the human qualities of an individual. A person's sense of himself and his ability to get along with others are the enduring elements that mean survival in the adult world. Yet we teach almost everything in life except how to get along with other people.

What it comes down to is figuring out what these young people want for themselves and how society can help them achieve their goals. When a group of adolescents with learning disabilities was canvassed a few years ago, their priorities came through very clearly. The Canadian Association for Children with Learning Disabilities has listed the first five this way:

1. Most of all I want to have a job and earn money.

2. Most of all I want to have family security.

3. Most of all I want a girlfriend (or boyfriend).

4. Most of all I want friends my own age.

5. Most of all I want schoolteachers who understand my learning problems.

The concerns of LD adolescents, then—and the solutions —are as typical and diverse as they are for all teenagers. But just as more attention must be paid to their educational needs, so must we attend to their social needs. The prognosis is good for those who have successful educational and social experiences. While they may not accomplish quite as much in life as they dream about, most certainly can succeed to a reasonable extent. With the strong support of family and school, LD adolescents can be well prepared for adulthood when they are ready to leave the nest.

chapter
9

IT DOESN'T *ALWAYS*
GO AWAY: THE LD ADULT

It is only in the past several years that LD adults have come
out of the closet. And it is only recently that the field itself
has acknowledged that a learning disability is not always
outgrown. Many LD children become LD adults either because they did not get appropriate help or because professional intervention was not successful. The present
generation of adults may not even have known what was
wrong as they suffered and struggled through years of school.
Their problems, in fact, may only have been identified long
after they left school—when their own children's learning
disabilities were diagnosed or when they saw a TV program
on the subject. Identification of learning disabilities is that
recent.

In the past few years, though, LD adults have banded
together in local groups across the country to share their
problems and search for solutions. Dale Brown, a vivacious
young woman with a learning disability herself, founded the
Association of LD Adults, a self-help group in the Washington, D.C., area, and coordinated the first national meeting in
1980.

In a recent article, Dale told of her reaction upon learning
that she did, indeed, have a learning disability. She said she
felt "strange, happy, upset, and relieved all at once." She
finally knew what had been the matter all those years, but the
future frightened her. After all, she had just been told for the

first time that she was "handicapped." This was a bitter pill to swallow, even though she might have suspected much worse.

Getting the facts is important since many adults still have to cope with the problems that plagued them earlier. It is not uncommon for reading and writing deficits to persist into adulthood—along with the concomitant social problems. And most people are far less understanding and tolerant of the socially clumsy adult than they are of the awkward child.

Imagine, for a moment, a child with learning disabilities who is disorganized and has a poor sense of time. She comes home late for meals and her room is a mess. As an adolescent, she has trouble getting term papers written on time, her room is worse than ever, and she is often unreliable or late for appointments. This adolescent grew up and is now a friend of mine. She is married and has a family (with two LD children), but she is still disorganized and gets so caught up in trivia that she cannot function efficiently. It takes her three times as long to get a chore done as it would anyone else. Her sense of timing hasn't improved either. She is a chronic procrastinator who started to plan her husband's birthday party only the day before the event. She knew she should have begun earlier, but she just couldn't mobilize herself. By the evening of the party, she was so anxious and exhausted, she didn't enjoy it at all. In addition, she forgot to invite some close friends, whose feelings were terribly hurt. The affair was a fiasco. It took a while before she could tell me the story and laugh at her own mismanagement.

Typical characteristics of many LD youngsters—immaturity, impulsiveness, poor judgment, and a lack of social perception—affect adults as well, and make it hard for them to live as others do. Independent living cannot always be taken for granted. In our society, the symbol of adulthood is leaving home. It is expected that a youngster finishing his education, whether at sixteen or twenty-one, will be on his own—to work, marry, travel, or whatever. For many with learning disabilities, though, the options may be limited.

Some stay at home with their families far beyond the teen years. Their schooling may take longer, their salaries are often low, and they may not have acquired the necessary life skills. So they are forced to remain in the family domicile, perhaps resented by parents and disdained by peers.

Though grown-up, they are still "children" in their own homes. As such, they lack the opportunities for a normal social life. Ernest Siegel* says it may take the LD person about five years to "catch up" before he can assume the role of the average non-handicapped individual of the same age.

Some adults who are severely impaired may always need a sheltered environment. Halfway houses, group homes, and sheltered workshops may be the answer for them. But regardless of their living situation, those with residual problems need to learn and practice social skills. Otherwise, they will be out of step wherever they are.

I recently met with a group of LD adults in their twenties and thirties. As I looked around at the men and women gathered for the first time, I realized they were united more by their social problems than by their poor academic skills. Although some had jobs and families of their own, most were still floundering, searching for a better life. Regardless of age or level of accomplishment, they all said they felt insecure socially and some were extremely lonely.

Most members of the group had been aware of their learning disabilities from a relatively early age, and certainly of their social problems as well. They recalled having felt "picked on" or "left out" as youngsters. Though they were no longer the scapegoats on the playground, those old feelings surfaced all too frequently. They wanted understanding and greater self-confidence—and hoped the group would help.

One of the issues we talked about was how to create a good first impression. One young woman said that she was usually

*Siegel, Ernest, *The Exceptional Child Grows Up.* New York: Dutton, 1974.

tongue-tied until she knew people well, so no one remembered she was around. Another said she talked too much out of nervousness and couldn't seem to stop herself. A man had been told by his wife that he interrupted when others were speaking and it was embarrassing. These surely are not exclusively LD problems, but they seem to be more common in this group.

How to make and keep friends was another major concern of the members. Too often, they felt they had missed a chance for a close relationship because of their fear of rejection. They were afraid that if others got to know them well, they would no longer be their friends. Many were self-conscious about their learning disabilities and tried hard to keep them secret. One woman had not even told her fiancé and needed advice about when and how to do this. She knew she should confess but couldn't quite figure out how.

Everyone in the group empathized with the engaged young woman. The issue of whether to tell people about their learning problems had concerned all of them at one time or another. There were those who refused to discuss their problems because they felt it made a difference in the way they were viewed by others, particularly on the job. Others felt strongly that they should tell friends and employers. They had found greater understanding when they did—when the timing was right. Their advice was "Don't discuss your learning disabilities until you're sure you've made a friend. Otherwise, you may scare people off."

The people in this group carried with them the shame and stigma that had been attached to their handicaps when they were young. Some of these attitudes have changed, though, with all the talk about learning disabilities in the past few years. Maybe as a result of having help earlier and getting greater understanding from their parents, today's children will feel more at ease with themselves when they are adults. Actually, I have heard many youngsters brag to their friends about "my tutor" or "my shrink." Perhaps by the time they are ready to enter the adult community, they will not be embarrassed by their learning differences and may even have become their own best advocates. Their coping skills will undoubtedly help them, even in the job market.

Employment, the group agreed, is probably the most basic problem of all for the LD adult. Without a job, self-esteem and a social life are impossible. Roger G., a disillusioned member of our group, had had four jobs in as many months. Just as he thought he was beginning to catch on to the routine of each job, he was fired for "working too slowly," "making too many mistakes," or generally being "unsatisfactory." He felt that his learning problems were to blame—and he was frustrated! "It's not fair," he said, "but what can I do about it?"

We had no easy answers for him. His slow rate of learning, his absent-mindedness, and his poor memory did make it hard for him to hold a job. Several in the group understood exactly what he was going through; they had had similar experiences themselves.

Mary L. had had a different work experience from Roger's. She usually did well in a new job for the first few months. Then, because she seemed competent, she would be given additional responsibility. This was usually more than she could handle, and inevitably she "flunked." She might have been content with her first assignment but found it hard to say "no" to a promotion. Only she knew she wasn't ready for it, but she didn't want to say so. And, always optimistic, she was more than willing to try. She told the group of having quit several positions in anticipation of being fired, or when the new responsibilities made her so nervous she got sick.

Unfortunately, many LD adults are not equipped or trained for work they would enjoy. They have to settle for much less than their ability would suggest—or are pushed into *more* responsible positions than they are capable of handling. As one employer once told me, "People with learning disabilities just don't fit in my corporation. They are either overqualified, underqualified, or unable to pass the test." That had to be an exaggeration, but it is true that job stability is not characteristic of this group. Maybe because they are not usually suited to their work, LD persons tend to become restless and find it difficult to make real commitments to their jobs. Their response may not be that different from the much younger LD students in the classroom whose teacher doesn't understand them. For both groups, special consideration and accommodations are often necessary.

Many of our group meetings were spent on the practical problems of getting along in life. Losing concentration while driving and getting lost because of a poor sense of direction can be frightening. The inability to help their children with homework or balance the family budget and the pressures associated with meeting new people were a few of the problems they shared. Solutions had to be found on an individual basis, to be sure, but everyone agreed that it took an enormous amount of energy—and ingenuity—to compensate for their disabilities.

At one point the group decided it was time to plan some social events for its own entertainment. Bowling was vetoed since several had never learned how. Dancing, too, was uncomfortable for some, and there was always the problem of finding partners. Finally, they decided to picnic in the park the following week.

Planning and organizing the day had its own social value. The phoning back and forth, getting together to fry the chicken, and packing box lunches provided almost as much fun as the event itself. One young woman said her phone had never been so busy before and she loved it. This was what she had missed as a teenager.

Cooking became an important part of the group's activities. A few who had never learned how because they lived at home and relied on others found cooking a worthwhile skill to have. They could ask friends for dinner and feel proud of their expertise. Being a good host can almost guarantee a more active social life. And besides, eating at home is less expensive than going to a restaurant, no small advantage these days.

Bicycle trips, picnics, and dinners are only a few of the activities possible for an adult LD group. One group I heard about sponsored a weekend retreat, devoted to acquiring social skills and new friends.

Certainly not all adults with learning problems suffer from social disabilities. Many have all the friends they want and are very well integrated in their communities. They don't need a group situation since they have figured out ways of coping on their own. Like Dale Brown, they have found their niches in spite of their difficulties. In my travels around the country, I have met several people with learning disabilities who were eager to tell me their stories. Most had struggled to learn as children, but they had made it. They might initially have been called retarded, emotionally handicapped, even schizophrenic, but no one called them names now. As adults they were still acutely aware of their learning problems, but they had made a place for themselves in spite of them.

May W. has her own radio program in a major city. She interviewed me when I was in town because of her personal involvement with learning disabilities. As a young child, she had been labeled "retarded" by the school, and later "emotionally disturbed." She quit school at the legal drop-out age of sixteen and worked at the local supermarket for the next few years.

Then, when she was twenty-two, she heard a radio program on dyslexia and suddenly realized, "That's me!" She said she was so excited she couldn't sleep, and early the next morning she called the station to find out where she could go for an evaluation. The diagnosis: dyslexia. The accompanying good news was that she was highly intelligent.

The results of the diagnosis gave her the courage to go back to school to pass the high school equivalency exam. From there, she enrolled in a part-time college program and even though she still has difficulty with some of her courses, the college is almost obligated to find alternatives for her because she has a learning disability. Section 504 of the Rehabilitation Act of 1973 prohibits discrimination because of a learning disability or other handicapping condition. In the end, my friend will probably graduate *because* of her learning disability, not in spite of it.

Bob P., a star salesman in his thirties, understood his learning problems only when his daughter was referred to the school psychologist in second grade. She manifested all the same problems he had. He had gotten through school mainly by cheating, he said, and he had managed to complete two years of college that way. As a result, he had developed into a pretty effective con man. Today, he is highly successful in business but still feels inadequate and thinks he is fooling the world much of the time. He is embarrassed that he can't write well and does so little reading. It also bothers him that he has to rely on his wife to keep him informed.

Bob has many emotional scars from his learning disabilities. He has had periods of therapy in his adult life, but he feels that no one really understands his particular problems. He is convinced that only someone who has had a learning disability or is familiar with the devastating effects of having one could know what he is going through.

Not everyone with persistent problems feels as Bob does, even when the problems seem far more serious. A man I saw recently has been the superintendent of a large highway department for twenty-five years, though he can't read or write a word other than his name. He obviously has other talents and abilities that have helped him compensate. He supervises a staff of thirty employees and handles his job well. His forceful personality and administrative ability have enabled him to manage despite his severe learning disabilities. The only time he ran into trouble was when he had to take a civil service exam for a promotion. But because of his learning disability, he was entitled to a "reader" and, of course, passed the test. I wasn't too surprised, incidentally, when I learned that two of this man's children have had

trouble in school. But they also have the unqualified understanding and support of their father.

Mrs. E., a mother of three brilliant, achieving daughters,
never told anyone that she could not read or write beyond
fifth-grade level. In fact, she couldn't even admit to me at
first that she had never finished high school. She was a true
"closet dyslexic." She had avoided her problems by getting
married immediately after she left school. "After all," she
said, "there was nothing else I could do. I certainly had had
enough of school and I wasn't fit for anything else."

As her family grew, her problems seemed even more profound. She couldn't help her children with homework and
she always waited until everyone was out of the house to
write a Christmas card or a letter. Then she'd pile up the
dictionaries around her—and cry.

When the children started to leave home, she really got
frightened. She had been a good mother, but that had been
her whole life. What was she to do now? At the age of
forty-two, with the help of a friend who was an educational
therapist, she finally found the courage to come to terms with
her disabilities, confess her secret to her family—and work
on her skills as well. She was living proof that it is never too
late to learn! When we last spoke, she was enthusiastically
taking business courses at a local community college. And
her daughters occasionally helped her with *her* homework.
It was, as she said, "a new life."

Mrs. E. illustrates so well what adults with learning problems would do well to have as their goals. The three that
follow could almost be considered a kind of manifesto.

1. Learn what your problem is and understand it, even if it
takes persistence to find out.

2. Look for and find ways to help yourself, whether at home,
on the job, or in the social world.

3. Develop a network from which to obtain the help of
others. (This can include a rap or self-help group, counselors,
family, and friends.)

With greater awareness of learning disabilities and more emphasis on helping the LD adult, the future should be brighter and more hopeful than it has been to date. We need to provide this population with an appropriate social education early in their lives so they will not become the lonely LD adults of the next generation. At the same time, we must educate people without handicaps to accept and appreciate this population more readily. Having survived trial by fire and learned from the experience, LD adults have much to share and something special to offer.

chapter
10

BECOMING SOCIALIZED: SUMMING UP

Becoming a socialized human being is a complex process. It may be especially so for those with learning differences. It is only the "medicine" of caring and responsive people that can transform the lonely LD child into an involved, self-assured adult.

As children grow, they rely on three major systems of support: the family, the school, and the peer group. Even if all three are not working well at the same time, each contributes to the growth of the individual. The family provides the child's first interpersonal connection. Holding and talking to an infant are the beginnings of social contact. The response the child gets from those around him eventually helps to form his self-image. Long before he goes to school, parents begin to teach social awareness, and these lessons continue throughout the child's life at home.

To foster social development, parents can:

1. Provide good social models for their children by their own behavior.

2. Talk about what is appropriate behavior so that a child understands what is expected of him.

3. Praise positive social behavior when it occurs.

4. Organize cooperative family activities and participation; foster a sense of responsibility.

5. Discuss interpersonal conflicts when they arise and suggest alternative ways of handling them.

6. Establish a level of communication with children so that their problems and concerns can be shared. Careful listening is as important as giving good advice.

7. Encourage social independence and self-reliance for the LD adolescent and young adult.

Once a child enters school, his world becomes a larger place. School provides an opportunity for social learning as well as academic skills. Social skills can be taught and ought to be an integral part of a school program. A comprehensive social curriculum includes the teaching of both social perception and social behavior. At every level, the school should promote communication skills, sensitivity to others, self-awareness, and self-control.

To achieve some of these goals, teachers can:

1. Organize cooperative rather than competitive classrooms. This has been demonstrated to promote academic achievement as well as social adjustment.

2. Use peer pairing and/or a buddy system when appropriate.

3. Provide discussion time for airing problems in class.

4. Plan rap sessions or peer counseling for older students.

5. Reward positive social behavior.

All children spend their lives as part of a peer group—even if it's a rejecting one. From early childhood throughout life, we join others in work and in play. For youngsters with learning differences, making friends may be the most difficult task of all. The adults in a child's life may have to help him gain access to individuals and groups that are right for him. Some of the ways to promote peer contact and interaction are:

1. Find local organizations that he can handle and that seem appropriate. Scouts, YMCAs, or local recreation programs provide experience with peers.

2. Encourage a youngster to pursue what he is best at. It will enhance his image with his contemporaries—and himself.

3. Arrange social contacts, even with "bait" if necessary. A well stocked refrigerator, a trip to the zoo or movies, may bring a reluctant playmate to visit.

4. Teach social games and skills (dancing, bowling, roller skating) to facilitate meeting peers.

5. Affiliate with local church groups that have youth programs. These can be catalysts for a social life.

And if the right peer group doesn't seem to exist, parents or young adults can form a group of their own—perhaps in consultation with their ACLD chapter or Orton Society (organizations designed to provide services and information about learning disabilities.) I have known several groups that have started this way and continued most successfully because they served a specific need.

There are vast differences among those with inadequate social skills, but all human beings have the same social needs —for acceptance, approval, and belonging. To help the person with learning differences make an adequate life adjustment, we must be concerned with the teaching of social skills. We cannot ignore the social side of learning disabilities.

Bibliography

BOOKS FOR ADULTS

Anderson, Laurel E., ed. *Helping the Adolescent with the Hidden Handicap.* (Los Angeles, Calif.: California Association for Neurologically Handicapped Children, 1976).

Bell, Ruth, et al. *Changing Bodies, Changing Lives* (New York: Random House, 1980).

Bellak, Leopold, ed. *Psychiatric Aspects of Minimal Brain Dysfunction in Adults* (New York: Grune & Stratton, 1979).

Boston Women's Health Book Collective, *Ourselves and Our Children* (New York: Random House, 1978).

Brehm, Sharon S. *Help for your Child: A Parent's Guide to Mental Health Services* (New York: Prentice-Hall, 1978).

Brutten, M., et al. *Something's Wrong with My Child* (New York: Harcourt Brace Jovanovich, 1973).

Dreyer, S. *The Bookfinder: A Guide to Children's Literature About the Needs and Problems of Youth* (Circle Pines, Minn.: American Guidance Service, 1977).

Enzer, Norbert B., ed., with Kenneth W. Goin. *Social and Emotional Development—The Preschooler* (New York: Walker & Co., 1978).

Gardner, Richard A. *MBD: The Family Book About Minimal Brain Dysfunction* (New York: Jason Aronson, 1973).

Gordon, Sol. *Living Fully: A Guide for Young People with a Handicap, Their Parents, Their Teachers, and Professionals* (New York: John Day, 1975).

———. *On Being the Parent of a Handicapped Youth* (Albany, N.Y.: NYALD, 1973). (paper)

Gordon, Thomas. *P.E.T.: Parent Effectiveness Training* (New York: New American Library, 1975).

Hawes, Gene R., et al. *How to Raise Your Child to Be a Winner* (New York: Rawson, Wade, 1980).

Kagan, Jerome. *The Growth of the Child: Reflections on Human Development* (New York: Norton, 1978).

Kranes, Judith Ehre. *The Hidden Handicap* (New York: Simon & Schuster, 1980).

Kronick, Doreen. *They Too Can Succeed* (San Rafael, Calif.: Academic Therapy Publications, 1969).

———. *A Word or Two About Learning Disabilities* (San Rafael, Calif.: Academic Therapy Publications, 1973).

McWhirter, J. Jeffries. *The Learning Disabled Child: A School and Family Concern* (Champaign, Illinois: Research Press, 1977).

Osman, Betty B. *Learning Disabilities: A Family Affair* (New York: Random House, 1979).

Ross, Dorothea M., and Sheila Ross. *Hyperactivity* (New York: John Wiley & Sons, 1976).

Rowan, Ruth Dinkins. *Helping Children with Learning Disabilities: In the Home, School, Church and Community* (Nashville, Tenn.: Abingdon, 1977).

Siegel, Ernest. *The Exceptional Child Grows Up: Guidelines for Understanding and Helping the Brain-Injured Adolescent and Young Adult* (New York: Dutton, 1974).

Siegel, Rita and Ernest. *Help for the Lonely Child: Strengthening Social Perceptions* (New York: Dutton, 1978).

Simpson, Eileen. *Reversals: A Personal Account of Victory over Dyslexia* (Boston: Houghton Mifflin Co., 1979).

Smith, Fred. *Parent Growth Through Group Experience: A Study Guide for Families of Children with Special Learning Needs* (San Rafael, Calif.: Academic Therapy Publications, 1976). (paper)

Smith, Sally. *No Easy Answers* (Cambridge, Mass.: Winthrop Publishers, Inc., 1979).

Stevens, Suzanne H. *The Learning-Disabled Child: Ways That Parents Can Help* (Winston-Salem, N.C.: John F. Blair, 1980).

Stewart, Mark. *Raising the Hyperactive Child* (Evanston, Ill.: Harper & Row, 1973).

Wallerstein, Judith S. and Joan Berlin Kelly. *Surviving the Breakup: How Children and Parents Cope with Divorce* (New York: Basic Books, 1980).

Weiss, Robert S. *Going It Alone* (New York: Basic Books, 1980).

Whitmore, Joanne Rand. *Giftedness, Conflict, and Under-Achievement* (Boston: Allyn and Bacon, 1980).

Yamamoto, Kaoru, ed. *The Child and His Image* (Boston: Houghton Mifflin, 1972).

Zimbardo, Philip G. *Shyness: What It Is, What To Do About It* (New York: Addison-Wesley, 1977).

BOOKS FOR CHILDREN

Albert, Louise. *But I'm Ready to Go* (Scarsdale, N.Y.: Bradbury Press, 1976).

Byars, Betsy. *The Summer of the Swans* (New York: Viking, 1970).

Chase, Francine. *A Visit to the Hospital* (New York: Grosset and Dunlap, 1977).

Cohen, Miriam. *Will I Have a Friend?* (New York: Collier, 1971).

Fassler, Joan. *One Little Girl* (New York: Behavioral Publications, 1969).

Gardner, Richard A. *The Boys and Girls Book About Divorce* (New York: Jason Aronson, 1971).

Kalb, Jonah and M. Viscott, *What Every Kid Should Know About Being Angry* (Boston: Sensitivity Games, Inc., 1977).

————. *What Every Kid Should Know About Feelings* (Boston: Sensitivity Games, Inc., 1976).

Lasker, Joe. *He's My Brother* (Chicago: Albert Whitman & Co., 1974).

Lobel, Arnold. *Frog and Toad are Friends* (New York: Harper & Row, 1970).

Silman, Roberta. *Somebody Else's Child* (New York: Frederick Warne, 1976).

Smith, Doris Buchanan. *Kelly's Creek* (New York: Crowell, 1975).

Sobol, Harriet Langsam. *Jeff's Hospital Book* (New York: Henry Z. Walck, 1975).

————. *My Brother Steven is Retarded* (New York: Macmillan, 1977).

————. *My Other-Mother, My Other-Father* (New York: Macmillan, 1979).

Stein, Sara Bonnett. *About Dying: An Open Family Book for Parents and Children Together* (New York: Walker, 1974).

Udry, J. M. *Let's Be Enemies* (New York: Scholastic Book Service, 1969).

Viorst, Judith. *I'll Fix Anthony* (New York: Harper & Row, 1969).

Wasson, Valentina P. *The Chosen Baby* (Philadelphia: J. B. Lippincott, 1950).

Wolf, Anna W. M. *Helping Your Child to Understand Death* (New York: Child Study Press, 1973).

PERIODICALS

ACLD Newsbriefs. Association for Children and Adults with Learning Disabilities, 4156 Library Road, Pittsburgh, Pa. 15234.

Common Sense. Closer Look, Box 1492, Washington, D.C. 20013.

The Exceptional Parent. 296 Boylston Street, Boston, Mass., 02116.

Gifted Children's Newsletter. 530 University Avenue, Palo Alto, Calif. 94301.

Perceptions, the Newsletter for Parents of Children with Learning Disabilities. P.O. Box 142, Milburn, N.J. 07041.

BOOKS AND MATERIALS TO WRITE FOR

A Directory of Summer Camps for Children with Learning Disabilities. ACLD, 4156 Library Road, Pittsburgh, Pa. 15234.

Clothing and Grooming Manual for Special Young Men, by Bebe Antell. Perceptions, P.O. Box 142, Milburn, N.J. 07041.

Directory for Exceptional Children. Porter Sargent Publishers, Inc., 11 Beacon Street, Boston, Mass. 02108.

Steps to Independence, by Dale Brown. Closer Look, P.O. Box 1492, Washington, D.C. 20013.

Facts About Sex for Today's Youth, by Sol Gordon. NYALD, 217 Lark Street, Albany, N.Y. 12210.

A Guide to Post-Secondary Education Opportunities for the Learning-Disabled. Time Out to Enjoy, Inc., 113 Garfield Street, Oak Park, Ill. 60304.

Directory of Facilities and Services for Learning Disabled (ninth edition, 1981–1982). Academic Therapy Publishers, 20 Commercial Blvd., Novato, Calif. 94947.

A Route to Independent Living: A Final Report. A.R.I.L./A.C. ACLD, 3851 North Upland Street, Arlington, Va. 22207 ($7.50).

Listing of Services for Post-Secondary LD Adult. Academic Therapy Publishers, 20 Commercial Blvd., Novato, Calif. 94945.

How to Get Services by Being Assertive, Coordinating Council for Handicapped Children, 407 South Dearborn, Rm. 680, Chicago, Ill. 60605 ($4.00 + 50¢ handling).

Guide for Administering Examinations to Handicapped Individuals for Employment Purposes, by Sandra Heaton, Anice Nelson, and Mary Ann Nester. U.S. Office of Personnel Management, Personnel Research and Development Center, Examination Services Branch, Washington, D.C.

Learning Disability: Not Just a Problem Children Outgrow. The President's Committee on Employment of the Handicapped, Washington, D.C. 20210.

A National Directory of Four Year Colleges, Two Year Colleges and Post High School Training Programs for Young People with Learning Disabilities (fourth edition, 1981), P.M. Fielding, ed. Partners in Publishing, P.O. Box 50347, Tulsa, Okla. 74150.

Appendices

EDUCATION FOR ALL HANDICAPPED CHILDREN
ACT—PUBLIC LAW 94–142

This revolutionary public law was enacted on November 29, 1975. It contains extensive amendments—some of which are the following:

1. To assure that all handicapped children have available to them a free appropriate public education.

2. To assure that the rights of handicapped children and their parents are protected.

3. To assist state and local public education systems in providing for the education of handicapped children.

4. To assess and assure the effectiveness of efforts to educate handicapped children.

This Act guarantees "that all handicapped children have available to them . . . a free appropriate education which emphasizes special education and related services designed to meet their unique needs." The law now *requires* that the school provide a suitable education at public expense. It also mandates that the public educational system must inform a parent of the procedures (termed *due process*) that he or she can follow to win such education under the law.

When a parent initiates a request for special help for his or her child, the school psychologist and/or assessment team conducts an evaluation. The law requires that a child's present level of performance be identified, that goals and objectives be set on the basis of assessed needs, and that services be provided in a setting designed to meet those needs.

REHABILITATION ACT OF 1973—"THE CIVIL RIGHTS ACT FOR THE HANDICAPPED"

In September, 1973, Congress passed a law that prohibits discrimination on the basis of physical or mental handicap in every active federally assisted program in the country. There are four sections of this Act which are of particular importance to the handicapped: Sections 501, 502, 503, and 504.

Handicap is defined in this Act as " . . . any impairment which substantially limits one or more of a person's major life activities."

Section 501 requires that federal agencies take affirmative action to hire and promote disabled persons.

Section 502 sets up a federal compliance board to make sure disabled persons have access to all buildings owned, occupied, or financed by the U.S. government.

Section 503 of the Rehabilitation Act deals with affirmative action obligations of contractors and subcontractors for handicapped workers. Contractors and subcontractors who receive government contracts are obliged to seek qualified handicapped individuals for employment and advancement.

Section 504 of this Act stipulates that handicapped people have the following rights:

- As disabled job applicants or employees they have the same rights and benefits as a non-handicapped applicant and employee.

- As disabled people, they are entitled to all medical services and medically-related instruction available to the public.

- As disabled people, they have the right to participate in vocational rehabilitation, senior citizen activities, day care (for disabled children) or any other social service program receiving federal assistance on an equal basis with non-handicapped.

- They have the same rights as anyone else to go to college or enroll in a job-training or adult post–high school basic education program. Their selection must be considered solely on the basis of their academic or other school records. Their disability is not a factor.

- State and local school districts must provide under Section 504 an appropriate elementary and secondary education for physically or mentally handicapped children. This public program must cost no more than it costs parents of non-handicapped children.

If you feel that your rights or those of your child have been violated because of a disability, write or call giving details to the Office for Civil Rights of the Department of Health, Education, and Welfare in your region, whose address is listed below:

Region I (Conn., Maine, Mass., N.H., R.I., Vt.)
140 Federal Street, 14th Floor
Boston, Mass. 02110

Region II (N.J., N.Y., Puerto Rico, Virgin Islands)
26 Federal Plaza, 33rd Floor
New York, N.Y. 10007

Region III (Del., D.C., Md., Pa., Va., W. Va.)
P.O. Box 13716
Philadelphia, Pa. 19101

Region IV (Ala., Fla., Ga., Ky., Miss., N.C., S.C., Tenn.)
101 Marietta Street, 10th Floor
Atlanta, Ga. 30323

Region V (Ill., Ind., Mich., Minn., Ohio, Wis.)
300 South Wacker Drive
Chicago, Ill. 60606
Or Cleveland, Ohio office, Region V:
Plaza Nine Building
55 Erieview Plaza, Room 222
Cleveland, Ohio 44114

Region VI (Ark., La., N.M., Okla., Texas)
1200 Main Tower Building
Dallas, Texas 75202

Region VII (Iowa, Kan., Mo., Neb.)
Welve Grand Building
1150 Grand Avenue
Kansas City, Mo. 64106

Region VIII (Colo., Mont., N.D., S.D., Utah, Wyo.)
Federal Building
1961 Stout Street, Room 11037
Denver, Colo. 80294

Region IX (Ariz., Calif., Hawaii, Nev., Guam, Trust Terr., Pac.
Isles, Amer. Samoa)
100 Van Ness Avenue, 14th Floor
San Francisco, Calif. 94102

Region X (Alaska, Idaho, Ore., Wash.)
1321 Second Ave., Room 5041 MS/508
Seattle, Wash. 98101

The Office for Civil Rights enforces federal laws prohibiting
discrimination against persons on the basis of race, color, national
origin, religion, sex, age, or mental and physical handicap and
investigates discrimination complaints brought by individuals
under these statutes.

Each year, more programs of higher education become available to those with learning disabilities. Because of federal legislation and a commitment to an educated society, an increasing number of colleges and universities are accepting and accommodating those with special needs. Some of the schools known to accept those with learning differences are listed here, but I would advise students seeking post–secondary school programs to extend their sights beyond this list. "Mainstreaming" applies to the college years too, and students who understand their problems and are willing to work hard may be able to handle greater challenges than they might have thought possible.

The following colleges and universities, listed by state, accept students with learning disabilities. The list was published, though not necessarily endorsed, by the Association for Children with Learning Disabilities (ACLD) as a service to parents and professionals.

ALABAMA

Daniel Payne College
Contact: Ms. Rea Trennen
Title III Coordinator
Daniel Payne College
2101 West Sayreton Road
Birmingham, Ala. 35214

Patrick Henry State Junior College (2 yr.)
Contact: John Lamkin
Patrick Henry State Junior College
Box 731
Monroeville, Ala. 36460

S. D. Bishop State Junior College (2 yr.)
Contact: Mrs. M. Dillard, Registrar
S. D. Bishop State Junior College
351 N. Broad Street
Mobile, Ala. 36603

Selma University (2 & 4 yr.)
Contact: Mrs. Ira Durgan, Director
Student Support & Special Program
Selma University
Selma, Ala. 36701

The University of Alabama
Contact: Charles J. Horn, Project Director
RETOOL—The University of Alabama
P.O. Box 2592
University, Ala. 35486

ARIZONA

Navajo Community College (2 yr.)
Contact: Mary L. Pettit
Director of Special Education
Navajo Community College
Tsaile, Ariz. 86556

Scottsdale Community College
Contact: Dr. G. Groenke, Chairman
Communications Studies
Scottsdale Community College
P.O. Box Y
Scottsdale, Ariz. 85251

Arizona State University
Contact: Ann Rispoli, Director
Arizona State University Special Services for Educational Opportunity
Tempe, Ariz. 83281

ARKANSAS

College of the Ozarks
Contact: C. D. Saddler, Ph.D., Director
Special Learning Center
College of the Ozarks
Clarksville, Ark. 72830

CALIFORNIA

Bakersfield College
Contact: Director of Counseling
Office of Student Services
1801 Panorama Drive
Bakersfield, Calif. 93305

Orange Coast College
Contact: Barbara Spear, Associate Dean
2701 Fairview Road
Costa Mesa, Calif. 92626
(714) 556-5651

Pasadena City College
Contact: Emy Lu Weller, Ph.D.
Special Services
1570 E. Colorado Boulevard
Pasadena, Calif. 91106
(213) 578-7127

California State University—Northridge
Contact: Jean Hutchinson
Assistant to the Dean
Admissions & Records
California State University
Northridge, Calif. 91324

College of the Redwoods (2 yr.)
Contact: Carl Lude, Dean
Student Special Services
College of the Redwoods
Eureka, Calif. 95501

Crafton Hills College (2 yr.)
Contact: D.A. Yowell
Crafton Hills College
11711 Sand Canyon Road
Yucaipa, Calif. 92399

Merced College (2 yr.)
Contact: Lynn Ireland
Program for Handicapped
Merced College
3600 "M" St.
Merced, Calif. 95340

Southwestern College (2 yr.)
Contact: Leon L. Stewart,
Counseling
Southwestern College
900 Otay Lakes Road
Chula Vista, Calif. 92010

The Devereux Foundation
Contact: Keith A. Seaton, Admissions Officer
The Devereux Foundation in
California
P.O. Box 1079
Santa Barbara, Calif. 93102

Sonoma State University
Contact: Office for Students
with Disabilities
Sonoma State University
Rohnert Park, Calif. 94928
(707) 664-2677

University of California—Fernald—L.A.
Contact: Linde Taylor
Mailing Address: 405 Hilgard
Avenue
Los Angeles, Calif. 90024
Street Address: 10620 Sunset
Boulevard
Los Angeles, Calif. 90024
(213) 825-2140
(A research & training setting
for children and adults)

College of the Sequoias
Contact: Susie Myers
Learning Assistance Center
915 S. Mooney Boulevard
Visalia, Calif. 93277
(209) 733-2050

Monterey Peninsula College
Contact: Nadine Davis
Monterey Peninsula College
980 Fremont Avenue
Monterey, Calif. 93940

The College of San Mateo
Contact: Mary Herman
College of San Mateo
1700 W. Hilldale Boulevard
San Mateo, Calif. 94002

Ventura Community College
Contact: Jeffrey Rd. Barsch
Ventura Community College
Ventura, Calif. 93003

Citrus College
Contact: Audrey Abas, LD
Specialist
Learning Assistance Center
18824 E. Foothill Boulevard
Azusa, Calif. 91720
(213) 335-0521, Ext. 373

City College of San Francisco
Contact: Rebecca Reilly, Coor-
dinator
Diagnostic Learning Center
50 Phelan Avenue, Rm. C-332
San Francisco, Calif. 94112

College of Alameda
Contact: Patricia Kerr, LD
Specialist
555 Atlantic Ave.
Alameda, Calif. 94501
(415) 522-7221

Napa College
Contact: Doug Dibble
Napa College
2277 Nap-Vallejo Highway
Napa, Calif. 94558
(707) 255-2100

San Jose City College
Contact: Martha Glazer, LD
Specialist
San Jose City College
2100 Moorpark Avenue
San Jose, Calif. 95128
(408) 298-2181, Ext. 246

Santa Ana College
Contact: Cheryl Dunn-Hoanzl
Coordinator—L.D. Program
Santa Ana College
Seventeenth at Bristol
Santa Ana, Calif. 92706
(714) 835-3000

CANADA

Connestoga College of Applied
Arts & Technology
Contact: E. Shurley Dickson,
Director
Connestoga College of Applied
Arts & Technology
Kitchener, Ontario, Canada

COLORADO

Adams State College
Contact: Neva Harden
Division of Humanities
Adams State College
Alamosa, Colo. 81102

El Paso Community College
Contact: Dr. Steven Walker,
Coordinator
Handicapped Program
2200 Bott Avenue
Colorado Springs, Colo. 80904

Lamar Community College (2
yr.)
Contact: Elaine Noccarato
Prescriptive Education
Lamar Community College
Lamar, Colo. 81052

Metropolitan State College
Contact: Eva Dyer, LD Program Development
Box 40, 1006 Eleventh Street
Denver, Colo. 80204
(303) 629-2533

Morgan Community College (2 yr.)
Contact: Janna Thiel
Morgan Community College
300 Main Street
Ft. Morgan, Colo. 80701

University of Northern Colorado
Contact: Mrs. Tedde Scharf
Office of Resources for the Disabled
Candelaria Hall 232
University of Northern Colorado
Greeley, Colo. 80639

University of Colorado
Contact: Laura Fischer, LD Coordinator
University of Colorado—Office of Services for Disabled Students
Willard Administration Center 18
Boulder, Colo. 80309
(303) 492-8932

Aims Community College
Contact: Donna Wright, LD Center
Aims Community College
P.O. Box 69
Greeley, Colo. 80631

CONNECTICUT

Central Connecticut State College
Contact: George Tenney, Coordinator
Special Services
Central Connecticut State College
1615 Stanley Street
New Britain, Conn. 06050
(203) 827-7652

Southern Connecticut State College
Contact: Natalie Bieber
Southern Connecticut State College
501 Crescent Street
New Britain, Conn. 06515

DELAWARE

Wesley College (2 Yr.)
Contact: Dr. Presley Hayes
Director of Counseling
Wesley College
Dover, Del. 19901

DISTRICT OF COLUMBIA

Southeastern University
Contact: B.D. McDowell
Southeastern University
501 I St., S.W.
Washington, D.C. 20024

FLORIDA

Central Florida Community
College (2 yr.)
Contact: Carolyn West
Central Florida Community
College
Box 1388
Ocala, Fla. 32670

Barry College
Contact: Dr. A. Sutton
Center for L.D.
Barry College
11300 N.E. Second Avenue
Miami, Fla. 33161

Fort Myers Junior College
Fort Myers, Fla. 33902

Miami Dade Community College
Contact: Charles Gonzales
Department of Developmental
Studies & Special Services
11380 N.W. 27th Avenue
Miami, Fla. 33167
(305) 685-4257

GEORGIA

Academy of Professional Drafting
Contact: Vida G. Roberts, Director
1655 Peachtree Street, N.E.
Atlanta, Ga. 30338

Andrew College
Contact: Morris G. Wray, Dean
Admissions, College Students
Andrew College
Cuthbert, Ga. 31740

Brandon Hall
Contact: Kenneth F. Stuckey
College Preparatory Coordinator
Brandon Hall
2500 Spalding Drive
Dunwoody, Atlanta, Ga. 30338

IDAHO

Lewis-Clark State College
Contact: Earl A. Loomis
Lewis-Clark College
Lewiston, Idaho 83501

College of Southern Idaho
Contact: Marvin Glasscock
College of Southern Idaho
Twin Falls, Idaho 83301

Ottumwah College
Ottumwah Heights, Idaho

ILLINOIS

University of Illinois
Contact: Division of Rehabilitation Educational Services
University of Illinois
Oak Street at Stadium Drive
Champaign, Ill. 61820

Southern Illinois University at
 Carbondale
Contact: Barbara Cordini
PROJECT ACHIEVE
Southern Illinois University
Carbondale, Ill. 62901

Lincoln College
Contact: Dean of Admissions
Lincoln College
Lincoln, Ill. 62656

Parkland College (2 yr.)
Contact: Louella Snyder,
 Learning Lab
Parkland College
2400 W. Bradley
Champaign, Ill. 61820

Harper Community College
Contact: Beverly Vaillancourt
Harper Community College
Palatine Ill. 60067
(312) 397-3000, Ext. 223

Barat College
Contact: Dr. Roger Faust,
 Dean of Admissions
Barat College
Lake Forest, Ill. 60045

Joliet Junior College
Contact: William Foss
Joliet Junior College
1216 Houbolt Avenue
Joliet, Ill. 60436

Kishwaukee College
Contact: Joseph J. Rembusch,
 Registrar
Kishwaukee College
Malta, Ill. 60150

Olivet Nazarene
Contact: Norman L. Moore,
 Director of Admissions
Olivet Nazarene
Kankakee, Ill. 60901

Quincy College
Contact: Joseph Quinn, Dean of
 Admissions
Quincy College
1830 College
Quincy, Ill. 63201

College of DuPage
Contact: Val Burke
College of DuPage
Lambert Road & 22nd Street
Glen Ellyn, Ill. 60137

Northwestern University
Contact: Dr. Jane Blalock
L.D. Center
Northwestern University
Evanston, Ill. 60201

INDIANA

Indiana University—Bloom-
 ington
Contact: Hila Kennedy, Coor-
 dinator
Services for the Handicapped
Student Health 347
Bloomington, Ind. 47405

University of Evansville
Contact: Director of Program
 Coordination
University of Evansville
500 Second Ave.
Evansville, Ind. 47710

Ball State College
Muncie, Ind.

IOWA

Coe College
Contact: Alan G. McIvor
Office of Admissions
Coe College
Cedar Rapids, Iowa 52402

Sioux Empire College (2 yr.)
Contact: Dr. A. D. Hudek
Sioux Empire College
Box 312
Hawarden, Iowa 51023

Wartburg College
Contact: Phyllis Schmidt
Director of Reading Center
Wartburg College
Waverly, Iowa 50677

KANSAS

Kansas Newman College
Contact: Sr. Aegidia Werth
Educational Laboratory
3100 McCormick
Kansas Newman College
Wichita, Kans. 67213

Kansas Technical Institute
Contact: Charles P. Scott, Director
Office of Student Affairs
Kansas Technical Institute
2409 Scanlan Avenue
Salina, Kans. 67401

KENTUCKY

Kentucky State University
Contact: Mrs. Hattie Duncan
Director of Special Services
Kentucky State University
Frankfort, Ky. 40601

LOUISIANA

The University of Southwestern
   Louisiana
Contact: Mr. James Caillier,
   Director
Special Services Program
University of Southwestern
   Louisiana
Lafayette, La. 70501

MAINE

Nasson College
Contact: Office of Admissions
Springvale, Maine 04083
(207) 324-5340

Southern Maine Vo-Tech Institute (2 yr.)
Contact: Gail Roberts, Coordinator
Developmental Studies
Southern Maine Vo-Tech Institute
Fort Road
So. Portland, Maine 04106

University of Maine—Farmington
Contact: Ed Nunery, Program of Basic Studies
University of Maine—Farmington
85 Main Street
Farmington, Maine 04938

MARYLAND

Community College of Baltimore (2 yr.)
Contact: Marvin Davis, Developmental Studies
Community College of Baltimore
2901 Liberty Heights Avenue
Baltimore, Md. 21215

Frostburg State College
Contact: Director, Student Special Services
Frostburg State College
207 Dunkle Hall
Frostburg, Md. 21532

Univ. of Maryland—Baltimore County
Contact: Dr. Virginia Redd, Director
Learning Resource Program
University of Maryland—Baltimore County
5401 Wilkens Avenue
Baltimore, Md. 21228

Montgomery Community College (2 yr.)
Contact: Lynne Harrison Martin, Coordinator
Programs & Services for Handicapped Students
Montgomery Community College
51 Mannakee Street
Rockville, Md. 20850
(301) 279-5058

MASSACHUSETTS

Curry College
Contact: Prof. Gertrude Webb
Curry College—Learning Center
Milton, Mass. 02186

Mount Wachusett Community College
Contact: Stephen A. Zona
Gardner, Mass. 01440
(617) 632-6600

American International College
Contact: Dr. Cynthia Hall
American International College
Springfield, Mass. 01109
(413) 737-5331, Ext. 420

MICHIGAN

Andrews University
Contact: Mrs. Marion Swane-
poel, Director
Freshman Activities
Andrews University Counsel-
ing & Testing
Berrien Spring, Mich. 49104

Mid Michigan Community Col-
lege (2 yr.)
Contact: Dr. Stanley J. Hergen-
roeder
Director, ILC
Mid Michigan Community Col-
lege
Harrison, Mich. 48625

Wayne County Community
College
4612 Woodward Avenue
Detroit, Mich. 48201

MINNESOTA

Minneapolis Drafting School
Contact: Robert Casserly, Di-
rector
Minneapolis Drafting School
3407 Chicago Avenue
Minneapolis, Minn. 55407

Normandale Community Col-
lege (2 yr.)
Contact: Dr. John Hilborn,
Dean
Normandale Community Col-
lege
9700 France Avenue S.
Bloomington, Minn. 55431

Hutchinson Area Vo-Tech Institute
200 Century Avenue
Hutchinson, Minn. 55350

MISSISSIPPI

Westminster College (2 & 4 yr.)
Contact: Admissions Office
Westminster College
Florence, Miss. 39073

Whitworth College
Contact: Mrs. Ira Mayfield
Whitworth College
Brookhaven, Miss. 39601

William Carey College
Contact: Antonio Pascals
Director of Admissions
William Carey College
Hattiesburg, Miss. 39401

MISSOURI

Westminster College
Contact: Mr. Henry Ottinger,
Director or
Mr. John Marshall, Dean of
Admissions
Westminster College
Fulton, Mo. 65251

Rockhurst College
Contact: Thomas J. Audley
Rockhurst College
5225 Troost
Kansas City, Mo. 64110

Missouri Southern State College
Joplin, Mo. 64801

Lindenwood College
St. Joseph, Mo.

MONTANA

Great Falls Commercial College
Contact: Denis Wingen, Director
Ebronix Learning Center
Great Falls Commercial College
905 First Avenue, N.
Great Falls, Mont. 59403

NEBRASKA

Doane College
Contact: Susan Snow
Reading & Learning Center
Doane College
Crete, Nebr. 68333

NEVADA

University of Nevada
Contact: Ms. Faith Reinhart
Counselor for the Handicapped
University of Nevada
Reno, Nevada 89507
(702) 784-6801

NEW HAMPSHIRE

Hesser College
Contact: J. Donovan Mills
Director of Admissions
Hesser College
155 Concord Street
Manchester, N.H. 03103

Nathaniel Hawthorne College
Contact: R. Raiche
Nathaniel Hawthorne College
Antrim, N.H. 03440

New Hampshire School of Electronics & Commerce, Inc.
Contact: Socrates Chaloge, President
New Hampshire School of Electronics & Commerce, Inc.
359 Franklin Street
Manchester, N.H. 03101

Clermont College
Clermont, N.H.

NEW JERSEY

Jersey City State College
Contact: Dr. Gary Spencer, Director
Learning Center
Jersey City State College
Jersey City, N.J. 07305

Bloomfield College
Bloomfield, N.J. 07103

NEW MEXICO

New Mexico Institute of Mining & Technology
Contact: Simon J. Gormuky
Director of Admissions & Financial Aid
New Mexico Institute of Mining & Technology
Socorro, N.M. 87801

Southwest College
Contact: JoAnn K. Bloom
Southwest College
525 San Pedro, N.E.
Albuquerque, N.M. 87108

NEW YORK

Brooklyn Public Library
Reading Improvement Program
Contact: Richard L. Keller,
Reading Improvement Program
Brooklyn Public Library
280 Cadman Plaza West
Brooklyn, N.Y. 11201

Jefferson Community College
Contact: John G. Phillips
Jefferson Community College
P.O. Box 473
Watertown, N.Y. 13601

The Brooklyn Center of Long Island University
Contact: Mr. Robert Nathanson
Special Educational Services
The Brooklyn Center
Long Island University
Brooklyn, N.Y. 11201

The Gow School (College Prep.)
Contact: David W. Gow
Headmaster, The Gow School
South Wales, N.Y. 14139
(716) 652-2371

The Russell Clinic
Contact: George J. Russell
The Russell Clinic
1417 Avenue P
Brooklyn, N.Y. 11229

Kalevala Tutoring School
Contact: Alti O. Tuomainen, Director
Kalevala Tutoring School
Maple Avenue
Philmont, N.Y. 12565

Adelphi University
Contact: Program for LD Students
Adelphi University, Eddy Hall
Garden City, N.Y. 11530
(516) 294-8700, Ext. 7555

State University of New York
—Binghamton
Contact: Office of Program for
Students with Disabilities
State University of New York
—Binghamton
Binghamton, N.Y. 13901
(607) 798-2686

State University of New York
—Farmingdale
Developmental College
Farmingdale, N.Y.

State University of New York
—Cobbleskill
Cobbleskill, N.Y.

Kingsboro Community College
Contact: Dr. Irwin Rosenthal,
Director
Kingsboro Community College
2001 Oriental Avenue
Brooklyn, N.Y.

New College at Hofstra University
Hofstra University
Hempstead, L.I., N.Y.

Marist College
Contact: Diane C. Perreira, Director
Office of Special Services
Poughkeepsie, N.Y. 12601
(914) 471-3240, Ext. 274

The Para-Educator Center for
Young Adults
New York University
Contact: Prof. Judith Kranes,
Director
PEC for Young Adults
School of Education, Health, &
Arts Professions
New York University
One Washington Place
New York, N.Y. 10003
(212) 598-3906

NORTH CAROLINA

Salem College
Center for Special Education
Contact: Dudley D. Shearburn,
Director
Winston-Salem, N.C. 27108
(919) 723-7961, Ext. 283, 284

Gardner-Webb College
Contact: Dr. Ralph Schoolcraft
Education Department
Gardner-Webb College
Boiling Springs, N.C. 28017

National School of Heavy
Equipment
Contact: Gene M. Collins
National School of Heavy
Equipment
P.O. Box 8529
Charlotte, N.C. 28208

NORTH DAKOTA

North Dakota State School of
Science (2 yr.)
Contact: James Horton, Director
Learning Skills Center
North Dakota State School of
Science
Wahpeton, N.D. 58075

North Dakota State University
Contact: Admissions Office
N.D. State University
Ceres Hall
Fargo, N.D. 58102

OHIO

Wright State University
Contact: Dr. Marlene Bireley
Wright State University
373 Millett Hall—LD Clinic
Dayton, Ohio 45435

Hobart School of Welding
Technology
Contact: Raymond Dunlavy
Supervisor, Student Affairs
Hobart School of Welding
Technology
Trade Square East
Troy, Ohio 45373

Sinclair Community College (2
yr.)
Contact: Robert Sattem
Sinclair Community College
444 W. Third Street
Dayton, Ohio 45402

University of Toledo
Contact: Office of Affirmative
Action
University of Toledo
2801 W. Bancroft Street
Toledo, Ohio 43606

OKLAHOMA

Oklahoma State University
Contact: Barbara Caldwell,
Ph.D.
Assistant Professor
Oklahoma State University
310 N. Murray Hall
Stillwater, Okla. 74074

Bacone College
Contact: Dr. Raymond Sewell
Bacone College
Muskogee, Okla. 74401

Oklahoma Baptist University
Contact: Paul Travis, Director
Trio Programs
Oklahoma Baptist University
Shawnee, Okla. 74801

Moore-Norman Vo-Tech
Contact: Bill Henderson
Moore-Norman Vo-Tech
School
4701 12th Avenue, N.W.
Norman, Okla. 73069

OREGON

Central Oregon Community College
Contact: R.R. Meddish, Registrar
Central Oregon Community College
Bend, Oreg. 97701

Lane Community College
Contact: Jim Ellison
Study Skills Learning Center
4000 East 30th Avenue
Eugene, Oreg. 97301

Willamette University
Contact: James Sumner, Admissions Office
Willamette University
Salem, Oreg. 97301

Portland Community College
Contact: Jan Zahler, L.D.
12000 S.W. 49th Avenue
Portland, Oreg. 97219

Mount Hood Community College
Contact: L.D. Teacher
Mount Hood Community College
26000 S.E. Stark
Gresham, Oreg. 97030

Eastern Oregon State
Contact: Dr. Bill Wells
Academic Reading Center
Eastern Oregon State College
Lagrande, Oreg. 97850

Portland State University
Contact: Mrs. Orcilia Forbes
Dean of Students
Portland State University
P.O. Box 751
Portland, Oreg. 97207

PENNSYLVANIA

New Castle Business College
Contact: Mr. Samuel Haycock
New Castle Business College
316 Rhodes Place
New Castle, Pa. 16101

Pennsylvania State University
Contact: Brenda G. Hameister, Coordinator
Services for Handicapped Students
Pennsylvania State University
Student Assistance Center
University Park Campus, 135 Boucke Building
University Park, Pa. 16802
(814) 863-2020

Breeden School of Welding
3578 MacArthur Rd.
Whitehall, Pa. 18052

Community College of Allegheny Co.
Mr. Peter Moshein
Allegheny Campus, CCAC, Rm. C324
808 Ridge Avenue
Pittsburgh, Pa. 15212

New Castle School of Trades
Contact: Joseph L. Clavelli
New Castle School of Trades
R.D. #1
Pulaski, Pa. 16143

St. Francis College
Contact: Dr. Joseph Bentivegna
Director, Educational Opportunity Center
St. Francis College
Loretto, Pa. 15940

SOUTH CAROLINA

Erskine College
Contact: Katherine B. Chandler
Program Director, Education Department
(803) 379-8867
or Roddy Gray, Admissions Office
Erskine College
Due West, S.C. 29639
(803) 379-8838

Aiken Technical College (2 yr.)
Contact: Judith Haskell, Supervisor
Basic Skills
P.O. Drawer 696
Aiken, S.C. 29801

Winthrop College
Contact: Mary A. Breakfield
Rehabilitation Act Coordinator
Winthrop College
113 Tillman Building
Rock Hill, S.C. 29733

SOUTH DAKOTA

Mount Marty College
Contact: J. Patrick Merrigan
Director of Admissions
Mount Marty College
Yankton, S.D. 57078

National College of Business
Contact: Guy Tillett
National College of Business
Box 1780
Rapid City, S.D. 57701

University of South Dakota
Contact: W. Michael Easton
Director of Student Affairs
University of South Dakota
University, S.D. 57006

TENNESSEE

Austin Peay State University
Contact: Dr. Al Bekus, Coordinator
Developmental Studies
Austin Peay State University
Clarksville, Tenn. 37040

Memphis State University
Contact: Jane Harrison
Department of Special Education & Rehabilitation
Memphis State University
Memphis, Tenn. 38152

Morristown College
Contact: Lanny R. Bowers
Morristown College
417 N. James Street
Morristown, Tenn. 37814

Trevecca Nazarene College
Contact: Mrs. Phyllis Flannery
Assistant Dean of the College
Trevecca Nazarene College
Nashville, Tenn. 37210

The University of Tennessee
Contact: Dr. W.E. Gaston
Assistant Dean of Admissions
305 Student Services Building
The University of Tennessee
Knoxville, Tenn. 37916

Tennessee Institute of Electronics
Contact: E.R. Massengill
Tennessee Institute of Electronics
3121 Broadway, N.E.
Knoxville, Tenn. 37917

TEXAS

Amarillo College
Contact: Access Center
Amarillo College
P.O. Box 447
Amarillo, Tex. 79109

Dallas Academy—Remedial School
Contact: Margaret S. Kroeger
Director of Admissions
Dallas Academy
950 Tiffany Way
Dallas, Tex. 75218

Lubbock Christian College
Contact: Director of Admissions
Lubbock Christian College
Lubbock, Tex. 79407

Project FIT
(Fundamental Industrial Training)
Contact: Dr. Elaine Adams
Project FIT, Tri-Co. Co-op
Commerce Public Schools
Commerce, Tex. 75428

San Antonio College (2 yr.)
Contact: Sharon Lynn Hill
Programs for the Handicapped
1300 San Pedro
San Antonio, Tex. 78284

San Jacinto College (2 yr.)
Contact: Dr. B. J. Honeycutt
San Jacinto College
8060 Spencer Highway
Pasadena, Tex. 77505

South Plains College (2 yr.)
Contact: Mr. Bill Powell
Guided Studies Program
South Plains College
Lovelland, Tex. 79336

Texas State Technical Institute
(Post H.S. Pre-Tech Training)
Contact: Howard Childs
Pre-Technical Study
James Connally Campus
Waco, Tex. 76705

Texas State Technical Institute
(Mid-Continent Campus)
Contact: Individual Skills Development Center
Texas State Technical Institute
Mid-Continent Campus
P.O. Box 11035
Amarillo, Tex. 79111

American Technological University
Contact: Ron Meek, Director of Admissions
American Technological University
P.O. Box 1416
Kileen, Tex. 76541

Gulf Coast Bible College
Contact: W. Maurice Slater
Director of Admissions
Gulf Coast Bible College
911 West 11th Street
Houston, Tex. 77008

Tarrant County Junior College
Contact: Joan Fernandes
Tarrant County Junior College
Northeast Campus
828 Harwood Road
Hurst, Tex. 76053

Texas State Technical Institute
(Rio Grande Campus)
Contact: Gene Campos, TSTI
P.O. Box 2628
Harlingen, Tex. 78550

Schreiner College
Contact: Julia Lacy
Schreiner College
Kerrville, Tex. 78028

East Texas State University
Contact: Mrs. Paula Ballew, Director
Mach III Special Services
East Texas State University
Commerce, Tex. 75428
(214) 886-5833

UTAH

Snow College (2 yr.)
Contact: Max E. Aycock
Learning Resource Center
Snow College
Ephraim, Utah 84627

Weber State College
Contact: LaMar C. Kap
Weber State College
3750 Harrison Boulevard
Ogden, Utah 84408

VERMONT

Johnson State College
Contact: David A. Crary
Johnson State College
Johnson, Vt. 05656

Southern Vermont College
Contact: Mr. James G. Dona-
hue, President
Southern Vermont College
Monument Road
Bennington, Vt. 05201

Ver-Shire Schools & Shops
Contact: George Coulter
NKMHS, Inc.
60 Broadview Avenue
Newport, Vt. 05855

Goddard College
Contact: Ms. Fran Toomey, Di-
rector
Special Education/M.A. Pro-
gram
Learning Skills Center
Plainfield, Vt. 05667

Pine Ridge School
(Remedial)
Contact: Director of Admis-
sions
Pine Ridge School
Box 138
Williston, Vt. 65495

VIRGINIA

Broadcast Academy of Rich-
mond
Contact: Karen Myers
Broadcast Academy of Rich-
mond
Suite 200, 2120 Staples Mill
Road
Richmond, Va. 23230

Paul D. Camp Community Col-
lege
Contact: Mrs. Collier
Paul D. Camp Community Col-
lege
Franklin, Va. 23851

Southern Virginia Community
College
Contact: Mr. John Sykes
Southern Virginia Community
College
Alberta, Va. 23947

Liberty Baptist College
Contact: Tom Diggs
Liberty Baptist College
P.O. Box 1111
Lynchburg, Va. 24505

Lord Fairfax Community Col-
lege (2 yr.)
Contact: Director of Admis-
sions
Lord Fairfax Community Col-
lege
Drawer E, U.S. Route 11
Middletown, Va. 22645

New River Community College
(2 yr.)
Contact: Mr. T.J. Anderson
Division of Developmental
Studies
New River Community College
Drawer 1127
Dublin, Va. 24084

Virginia Intermont College
Contact: Mrs. Margaret Crumley
Virginia Intermont College
Bristol, Va. 24201

WASHINGTON

Fort Steilacoom Community College
Contact: Pearl M. Rose
Occupational Education Office
Fort Steilacoom Community College
9401 Farwest Drive S.W.
Tacoma, Wash. 98449

Walla Walla Community College
Contact: Mrs. Hilda Thompson
Coordinator of Developmental Education
Walla Walla Community College
500 Tausick Way
Walla Walla, Wash. 99362

Bellevue Community College (2 yr.)
Contact: Nil Molvik, Chairman
Individual Development Division
Bellevue Community College
3000 S.E. Landerholm Circle
Bellevue, Wash. 98007

Clark College (2 yr.)
(Post H. S. Training)
Contact: Phil deGrood, Coordinator
Special Educational Services
1800 E. McLaughlin Road
Vancouver, Wash. 48663

Everett Community College (2 yr.)
Contact: W.J. Deller
Dean of Students Office
Everett Community College
801 Wetmore
Everett, Wash. 98201

Olympic College (2 yr.)
Contact: Ronald Cressland
Dean of Instruction
Olympic College
Bremerton, Wash. 98310

Seattle Central Community College (2 yr.)
Contact: Stanley R. Traxler
Seattle Central Community College
1718 Broadway
Seattle, Wash. 98122

Yakima Valley College (2 yr.)
Contact: Ms. Gaye Hickraw
General Tutorial Service
Yakima Valley College
P.O. Box 1647
Yakima, Wash. 98907

WEST VIRGINIA

West Virginia State College
Contact: Dr. Kurt Hofman
Provost of Student Affairs
West Virginia State College
Institute, W.Va. 25112

Bethany College
Contact: Barbara J. Divins
Assistant Professor/Education
Bethany College
Department of Education
Bethany, W.Va. 26032

West Virginia University
Reading Laboratory
719 College Avenue
Morgantown, W.Va. 26505
(304) 293-4997

WISCONSIN

Lakeland College
Contact: Director of Admissions
Lakeland College
Sheboygan, Wis. 53081

Gateway Technical Institute
(Post H.S. Training)
Contact: Barbara Greene
GTI Student Development
Center
1001 S. Main Street
Racine, Wis. 53403

Milwaukee Area Technical College
(2 yrs. & Post H.S. Training)
Contact: E. K. Hansen
MATC, 1015 N. Sixth Street
Milwaukee, Wis. 53203

Mount Senario College
Contact: Mr. Max Waits
Director of Admissions
Mount Senario College
Ladysmith, Wis. 54848

Northeast Wisconsin Technical
Institute
(Post H.S. Training)
Contact: Henry A. Wallace, Jr.
Student Services
Northeast Wisconsin Technical
Institute
2740 W. Mason Street
Green Bay, Wis. 54303

University of Wisconsin—Madison
Contact: Handicapped Student
Counseling
University of Wisconsin
1 South Park Street
Madison, WI 53706
and/or McBurney Resource
Center for Persons with
Disabilities
77 Bascomb Hall
Madison, Wis. 53706

University of Wisconsin—Stevens Point
Contact: Dr. John Larsen
Director of Admissions
University of Wisconsin—Stevens Point
Stevens Point, Wis. 54481

University of Wisconsin—Stout
Contact: David A. McNaughton
University of Wisconsin—Stout
Menomonie, Wis. 54751

University of Wisconsin—Whitewater
Contact: John Truesdale
University of Wisconsin—Whitewater
800 W. Main Street
Whitewater, Wis. 53190

University of Wisconsin—Oshkosh
Contact: Dr. Robert Nash
University of Wisconsin—Oshkosh
Oshkosh, Wis. 54901

WYOMING

University of Wyoming
Contact: Special Services Director
University of Wyoming
University Station, Box 3808
Laramie, Wyo. 82071

In order to increase communication among adults with learning disabilities, the National Network of Learning-Disabled Adults has developed a list of self-help and advocacy groups for learning-disabled adults.

All of the groups on this list have given permission to be included. They have stated that they meet the following criteria:

1. They have three or more people and meet regularly.

2. They are willing to take in new members.

3. They primarily serve learning-disabled adults.

ARKANSAS

Arkansas ACLD Adult Committee
c/o Charlotte Johnson
714 North 19th Street
Fort Smith, Ark. 72901
(501) 783-3873 (H)

CALIFORNIA

The Puzzle People
c/o Jo Anne Haseltine
122 Belvedere Drive
Mill Valley, Calif. 94941
(415) 388-4236 (H)

(No official name)
c/o Sally Hedberg
52 Overhill Rd.
Orinda, Calif. 94563
(415) 254-1010
After 3

COLORADO

Metropolitan Denver LD Adults Group
c/o Hal Ewoldt
1062 Josephine #7
Denver, Colo. 80206

CONNECTICUT

LD Adult Committee
c/o Mrs. Joellen Doyle
45 Longmeadow Hill Road
Brookfield, Conn. 06804
(203) 775-4583

GEORGIA

Georgia Association for Adults with Learning Disabilities
c/o Richard Kaplan
475 Burgandy Court
Stone Mountain, Ga. 30087
(404) 498-1606 (H)

ILLINOIS

Chicago Area Chapter
Time Out to Enjoy
c/o Dian Ridenour
113 Garfield Street
Oak Park, Ill. 60304

IOWA

Iowa Youth and Adult Group
Iowa ACLD
c/o Tom Potter
1003 Cadam Court
Cedar Falls, Iowa 50613
(319) 277-3519 (H)

Division of Youth and Adults
Iowa ACLD
c/o Donna Liscum
2617 N. 15th Place
Fort Dodge, Iowa 50501
(515) 573-3757

MARYLAND AND DISTRICT OF COLUMBIA

Association of Learning Disabled Adults
PO Box 9722
Friendship Station
Washington, D.C. 20016
Gale Bell
(301) 593-1035 (H)

MASSACHUSETTS

Friends of the Sensorially Deprived
c/o Pearl Rosborough
P.O. Box 186
Belmont, Mass. 01278
(617) 484-0340 (H)

Massachusetts Association of Learning Disabled Adults
c/o Bob Fahey
124 Morrison Avenue
Somerville, Mass. 02144
(617) 623-8874 (H)

Massachusetts Association of Learning Disabled Adults
c/o Maria Bacigalupo
Curry College
Milton, Mass. 02186

MINNESOTA

LD Youth/Adult Group
Minnesota ACLD
494 N. Griggs Midway Building
1821 University Avenue
St. Paul, Minn. 55104
(612) 646-6136

Minnesota ACLD Adult Committee
c/o Christine Hunter
616 S. Smith
St. Paul, Minn. 55107

(no official name)
c/o William Hawk
ELDA Reading and Math Clinic
III East Franklin Avenue, Suite 256
Minneapolis, Minn. 55404
(612) 871-9011 (W)

(no official name)
c/o Karen "Kandy" Schaeffer
7385 Arlington Drive
St. Louis, Mo. 63117
(314) 781-3476 (H)

Adelphia Learning Disability Group
c/o Nonnie Star, MSW
Adelphi University
Garden City, L.I., N.Y. 11530
(516) 560-8060 (W)
(516) 374-9285 (H)

Adult Consumer Committee
NYALD
217 Lark Street
Albany, N.Y. 12210
(518) 436-4633

Student Dyslexia Group
c/o Joe Trapp
The Ohio State University
1971 Neil Avenue
Columbus, Ohio 43210
(614) 891-1990 (H)
Alternative contact person:
D. Sostrum
(614) 262-9635 (H) after 6 P.M.

Learning Disabled Adult Committee
Ohio ACLD
4601 North High Street
Columbus, Ohio 43214
(614) 267-7040

Pennsylvania Youth and Adult Organization
c/o Mike Moeller
Treasurer
14 Race Avenue
Lancaster, Pa. 17603
(317) 397-7244 (H)

TEXAS

LAUNCH, Inc.
c/o John Moss
Department of Special Education
East Texas State University
Commerce, Tex. 75428
(214) 886-5932 (W)
Alternative contact person:
Linda Larch
(214) 886-5932

Texas ACLD
Virginia Kurko
548 N. Ollie
Stephenville, Tex. 76401
(817) 968-9096 (W)
(817) 965-4098 (H)

VIRGINIA

Division of Adults and Youth
Virginia ACLD
c/o Justine Maloney
P.O. Box 1255
Arlington, Va. 22210
(703) 243-2614

(no official name)
c/o Barbara Given
George Mason University
4400 University Drive
Fairfax, Va. 22030
(703) 323-2676 (W) between 9
    AM and 12 PM Monday
through Friday

Index

ABOUT THE AUTHOR

BETTY B. OSMAN is a specialist in learning disabilities. She is adjunct professor at Manhattanville College and lectures widely throughout the country. A graduate of Vassar College with advanced degrees from Teachers College at Columbia University, Ms. Osman lives in Scarsdale, New York, with her husband. She has three grown children.